Business Predators

Business Predators

How *Not* To Get Ripped Off in Small Business

Carla Carr

Library and Archives Canada Cataloguing in Publication

Carr, Carla, 1956-
Business predators : small business fraud and other risk issues / Carla Carr.

ISBN 978-1-897178-81-2

1. Small business--Security measures. 2. Fraud--Prevention. 3. Identity theft--Prevention. I. Title.

HD61.5.C37 2009   658.4'7   C2009-901094-1

The publisher gratefully acknowledges the support of the Department of Canadian Heritage through the Book Publishing Industry Development Program.

Printed and bound in Canada

Insomniac Press
520 Princess Ave., London, Ontario, Canada, N6B 2B8
www.insomniacpress.com

Contents

Introduction

Fraud artists cost small business owners millions of dollars per year in Canada—is your business safe from predators?

Are you a new small business owner? If so, then the information in this book is a basic necessity. I've written it to help business owners recognize that if they don't have a detailed fraud and risk strategy in place before they open their doors for business, they may be making their first costly management mistake. As a business owner it's important to understand this critical subject and have safeguards in place to protect your assets. Even if your company has been in operation for several years, you might not realize that every day countless established businesses fall prey to some very simple scams. There doesn't seem to be an end to the ingenuity being used to try to relieve you of your hard earned money. If you are not prepared, the next time a business is defrauded it might be yours! Find out what all the big companies already know.

If you don't think a book on small business fraud and risk is essential reading, I wish I could introduce you to the well-established and successful businesswoman I know who lost more than $100,000 to a bookkeeper over a three-year period. If she had had the knowledge that this book contains, the bookkeeper never would have gotten away with so much of her money. By finding out how he did it and putting precautions in place, you can make sure it never happens to you. (For the full story on what happened to him and how, see Chapter 4 on Accountants, Bookkeepers, and Lawyers.)

I have been employed in the financial services industry for over 30 years. When I first started working, banking was certainly much simpler than it is today. Back then I remember that everyone had two personal accounts: savings and chequing. Businesses had only one. There was no such things as completing your everyday banking at a branch other than the one where you had your account. There were no automated teller machines, no Internet banking, and no debit cards. I have seen this industry change dramatically since then. A Canadian Bankers Association survey "Taking a Closer Look: Technology and Banking" published in August 2006 indicates that only 29% of clients continue to visit their bank in person. In fact, 65% now exclusively use the various electronic forms available for all of their banking needs. I suspect that percentage is even higher today. That being said, there is a flip side to these modern conveniences. Bank services that were once simple have become more complicated— especially with several new government laws that are now in place, such as Canada's *Proceeds of Crime (Money Laundering) and Terrorist Financing Act*. In addition, with so many transactions now happening electronically, there has been a massive increase in the amount of frauds attempted against both individuals and businesses. Today's small business fraud is no longer just about a customer writing you a bad cheque. After spending 20 years working with business bank clients as an account manager and advisor, my current position entails managing fraud, risk, and compliance issues. I have seen and been involved in many unfortunate situations where someone has lost a lot of money, and, in some cases, their entire business, because of fraud. I would like to offer you some insight into the current and growing complexity of small business fraud.

Inventive and daring thieves continue to look for new opportunities. Fraud has become an enormously lucrative enterprise for scam artists all over the world. Are you aware of how effortlessly a thief, in an entirely different country, can steal your money? Could you be fooled? What about your staff? Have they been trained properly to recognize and avoid fraud? Business fraud is on the rise and continues to happen to many trusting and unprepared business people—take steps to ensure it doesn't happen to you.

About 98% of all businesses operating in Canada are small to mid-sized. They are our most important job creating group. Scammers are taking the honest small business owner's hard-earned money: Educating owners about vulnerabilities to fraud is important.

In addition to detailing many of the current business scams in operation, this book offers general risk awareness information for all types of business. Each chapter presents various business risk issues and safeguards that can be introduced to protect yourself and your livelihood.

If you already own and operate a successful company, getting up-to-date information on scams that target small business should be an ongoing priority. If you are just starting out, this is essential reading.

Important: If your business is currently dealing with a potential fraud situation and you require some guidance, please contact a professional accountant, banker, or lawyer for advice. Having a team of reputable experts available that understands your business should be a part of every small business strategy.

1.

Starting up: Important Issues to Consider Before You Open for Business

What you don't want to happen

I'd like to tell you about three young children, none older that 21, who were left struggling to hold onto a sizable family business after both parents became ill and died within one year of each other. Their parents had initially set up a $250,000 joint life insurance policy in the early stages of planning the business. They wanted to ensure the company, and ultimately their family, would have some financial protection in the event of either of their deaths. They knew that if anything happened to them the survival of the business would be dependent upon having at least two fully qualified individuals to carry on: one to complete the daily on-site operational requirements and the other to handle the sales, bookkeeping, and additional financial management. If something were to happen to one of them the ability for the business to continue would depend on someone stepping in very quickly to carry out these critical daily responsibilities. The life insurance would allow some funds to hire someone to fulfill either of the roles until one of the children could assume a managerial position. If necessary the funds could also provide some financial assistance to allow some time for the business to be sold for a reasonable price or be wound down if none of the three were able to take over.

The life insurance policy the parents had purchased had been in place nearly 20 years with the payments being made faithfully every month; however, the policy had not been reviewed since the day it was purchased. When they initially became ill neither of them contacted the insurance company to discuss their situation. No claim was made against the insurance policy until both parents had passed away. When the insurance company received the payout request they reviewed the policy, as is their usual practice. They determined that the business should have been paying additional premiums because one of the parents was a smoker. The insurance policy had not been properly set up right from the beginning. The increased premiums for being a smoker would have had to have been paid from the onset of the policy. As a result this one oversight alone resulted in the life insurance death claim being denied. Due to the error, the insurance company did agree to refund all of the premiums improperly collected for the past 20 years. Unfortunately, the funds received were not close to what the payout would have been if the policy had been accurately set up.

The three children, even with the assistance of relatives, were unable to continue operating the business on their own. They could not come up with sufficient funds to hire skilled employees to continue to operate the company until an alternate solution could be found. The business folded within a year.

This was a very unfortunate situation where failure to monitor life insurance policies caused the denial of a claim that would have made the children's lives much easier.

What you do want to happen

In a different case, having adequate life insurance in place went a long way toward helping a business owner's young family.

David was a very strong-minded and successful business owner, who managed a home maintenance work crew of 15 to 20 on a daily basis. Though he had always been healthy and was used to outdoor exercise, a very aggressive cancer was discovered when he was only in his mid 30s. He was initially very positive about the outcome of his disease, but unfortunately he passed away within six months of being diagnosed.

His wife Tina was a stay-at-home mother with three children under the age of ten. Losing her husband was difficult enough, and now she had to juggle the needs of her young family and learn to run David's business, too. Where else was the family's income to come from? She began by talking with her husband's bank business account manager. She was happy to know that the company that he had incorporated would still be able to run despite his death. She was officially on the bank account as the business' secretary and was able to continue operating the account. In addition, an enormous weight was lifted off her shoulders when she learned all of his business banking loans were covered by a life insurance policy. She was able to complete the insurance claim and receive payment within 45 days. The funds allowed her the time to see if she could continue to run the operation. She was successful in doing so. Unfortunately, we can never know what our fate will be or when it will arrive.

Make sure any life or health insurance applications are completed with accurate information. Be sure also to review your policies periodically to ensure that the coverage you have in place remains adequate for you and your family situation.

There are many issues to consider when making the decision to start up a new business, in order to choose the path that best suits your specific circumstances. In addition to an insurance professional, both an accountant and a business legal expert should be consulted. Here is a limited look at some options you should consider:

TYPES OF BUSINESS REGISTRATIONS

Sole ownership/Sole proprietorship

- Provincially registered.
- Business is owned by only one person, net income is taxed as an individual.
- The owner is personally liable for the business and its operations.

Partnership

- Provincially registered.
- Two or more persons engaged in a business enterprise. The partners can be active, in which case net income is split as per the business partnership agreement and taxed as an individual. Partnerships can also have "limited" partners that do not participate in the business operations but are investors only. Any income a limited partner earns is considered investment income.
- All persons are personally liable for the business and its operations, with the exception of limited partners who are liable only up to the amount of the funds they have invested.

Incorporation

- Provincially or federally registered.
- The business can be owned by one or more persons. An incorporated company is considered under law to be an "individual."
- The company itself files its own tax return and is taxed

on net income (with special income tax reductions for small businesses). The company owner(s) can draw wages, which are deducted as an expense by the company, then taxed for the individuals. Company owners also have the ability to withdraw all of their initial "equity" (cash injections) in the business with no tax consequences.

- The persons owning/operating the business are not considered personally responsible for the operations or debts of the company (unless proved personally responsible in a court of law).

SOLE OWNERSHIP ISSUES AND RISKS
Insurance Coverage

The two stories used to introduce this chapter hopefully demonstrated the need for everyone to investigate their insurance situation. Health insurance, critical illness or disability insurance, and life insurance are a few options. Consult with a life and health insurance professional to determine what is needed for your specific situation. You will need to estimate your monthly business income and operating costs, including your own personal expenses plus what it would cost to hire someone to replace you if you were not able to work. Even if you have not opened shop yet, this financial information should be available from your business start-up financial plan. Generally a business will change and adapt to market conditions as time goes by, therefore a review of life and other insurance protection is warranted every few years.

You should especially also review your coverage anytime there are significant changes in your business or personal life such as:

- marriage
- buying a new home
- having children (and sending them to college or university)
- divorce
- taking on the responsibility of aging parents
- retiring

If you have important personal financial responsibilities, as many of us do, your family may need this financial assistance to survive should something happen to you.

If you have a spouse you should also consider life insurance for them. Although your spouse may not be a partner in the business, if you have children would you be able to work and cope with a young family by yourself?

There are other insurances that will be required depending on the type of business you will be operating: business equipment and motor vehicle insurance, coverage for theft of inventory, stock or office equipment, and fire insurance policies for any commercial buildings you may own. You may also consider business interruption coverage. Business interruption insurance can be purchased as "gross earnings insurance" or "gross profits insurance." One covers losses occurring from the loss of production and the other covers the loss of sales. In both cases some type of accident must have occurred which caused the business to suffer a loss of income. Loss of production insurance only covers losses that occur until the production line is repaired or replaced. Loss of sales insurance covers financial shortfalls that continue to occur after production is resumed. Under this particular policy you could be paid for up to 12 months until your business income has recovered to the level it was prior to the production breakdown.

Business interruption insurance would be valuable to cover potential losses resulting from many different types of circumstances (only those that are beyond your control) that will last for several days, weeks, or months. This could include:

• breakdown of manufacturing equipment where parts/service or replacements are not immediately available
• flood, fire and other natural disasters that damage business equipment or property in such a way that the business cannot operate until repairs are made

The insurance does not normally cover the cost of fixing or repairing the equipment or buildings, it may only replace any lost income you will not be receiving while you are unable to generate sales. An insurance agent will advise you of coverage limitations and the situations that your policy will cover.

In addition to the possibility that you may one day be unable to work, your business could also suffer due to the loss, theft, or damage of equipment, vehicles, or inventory. If this should occur and the problems cannot be quickly corrected, significant income losses could result which may severely curtail your operations. Over an extended period of time, these types of issues could also cause a loss of clients, which may be difficult to recover.

Taxes

Income from a sole ownership is taxed as an individual after general expenses are deducted. General business expenses can include:

- employee wages and benefits
- rent or business property mortgage costs
- business taxes including GST and provincial sales taxes
- heat, hydro, telephone, Internet
- bank fees
- interest on business loans
- advertising
- accounting/bookkeeping
- costs of manufacturing materials
- business vehicle costs (licence plates, gas)

Death of the business owner

Further to the issue of life insurance coverage, you should be aware that a sole ownership ceases on death, with business assets becoming part of your general estate. You should have a suitable will in place if you intend for the business assets to be conveyed, intact, to a specific person.

Even if you have a proper will in place, if you should die your business activities cannot be continued by someone else. In addition, no one will be able to operate or have access to your business bank accounts, even if they previously had a power of attorney to sign. The person who inherits the business assets must register a new business in their own name and set up a new account. It is possible to have a power of attorney for a sole proprietorship because a business registered as such is legally one and the same as the owner. It does not matter whether the business is operated under their own personal name or under another chosen name i.e., Brian's Upholstery. Since there are no other partners in this type of business, it is reasonable for an independent individual to represent the sole business owner in decision making—if necessary.

GENERAL PARTNERSHIP/LIMITED PARTNERSHIP ISSUES AND RISKS

Legal agreements

It's especially important when starting up a partnership that a legal partnership agreement is drawn up by a lawyer before the business begins operation. Just registering a business name as a partnership with the government is not enough to protect each of you. Each partner needs to have a clear understanding of how the partnership will function in order to answer questions such as, what happens if one wants to leave and the other wishes the business to continue? The agreement will also outline other issues like:

- each partner's equity contribution or investment, including how and when they can withdraw it from the business;
- the purpose of the business and what each partner's responsibility is within it;
- the operation and management of the business assets, including the bank account;
- setting of salaries and bonuses;
- retiring or selling shares to an outsider; and
- dispute mediation.

Many partnerships do not survive more than a couple of years, even genial family-based ones. It's much different to work day after day with a family member or friend than to have only a familial or social relationship with them. Legal partnership agreements are worth their cost when drawn up before the business starts. There are many issues that can cause a business to fail and not having a proper partnership agreement in place can facilitate such a failure.

Additional life insurance coverage

What if one of the partners dies? How critical will the loss of that person be? And remember the portion of the business that the deceased owns now becomes part of his/her estate. You could end up with a brand new partner that you may not want to work with. Along with personal insurance to protect your family (as noted previously), a partnership should consider the purchase of additional life insurance for each of the partners. That way if one dies the insurance can cover the cost of the remaining partner(s) "purchasing" the others proportional share of the business assets from their estate. This is also called "key persons" insurance.

Legal liability

There is something else many persons forming new partnerships are not always aware of. If you are a "general" partner, each of you is legally responsible for 100% of the business debts, contracts, or other liabilities of the partnership. Even if you are only a 50% or 10% owner your percentage of ownership is irrelevant. How well do you know your partner(s)? You could be held equally financially responsible, if in the course of doing business another partner becomes liable for damages or injury to a client or to a client's premises. Only if you are a "limited" partner does this not apply. Limited partners are equity investors only and are not part of the daily business operations. They can only lose the funds they have invested. They are not personally responsible for any additional business debts.

CORPORATION ISSUES AND RISKS
Legal agreements

Just as for a partnership, corporations need to have a shareholder agreement to outline, in detail, the business operating terms, including each owner's responsibilities and rights. In the case of an incorporated company, the business does not cease on the death of a shareholder. For that reason, the incorporation document should outline what occurs when a shareholder passes away should an outside person or their estate become an owner of shares of the business.

An incorporated company is considered a separate legal entity. For the shareholders there is generally no personal liability for the business activities except under the following general conditions:

- a personal guarantee* is signed (often required for business borrowing through a bank); or
- if the business owner is legally found to have been personally negligent with respect to specific business transactions.

Business owners who set up or change their company shareholdings to include children under the age of 18 (for estate planning purposes) should consult a lawyer before doing so. There are specific regulations to be followed with regards to children owning a stake in a corporation. You should also be aware that in order to open a business account at a bank all shareholders owning 10–25% or more must usually sign the account opening documents, regardless if they will be an actual signing authority or not. As all persons signing for a business bank account must be at least 18 years of age, under the circumstances it would seem practical to inquire with your bank the percentage of ownership that is required to sign new or to change existing accounts before you legally register any such ownership changes. You will need to ensure that underage children who become company shareholders should each own less than the prescribed amount since, as minors, they will not be able to sign bank account documents. If you make these changes without legal or bank consultation you may not be able to operate your business account.

As an example, there was a situation that I dealt with where a professional had an incorporated business that he owned with his wife. He paid for and registered a change of ownership with the provincial government where he added his two young children as lesser owners. Both were under the age of 18. One of the reasons someone may do this is that if the parent(s) die, the business assets automatically become owned by the remaining partners without estate taxes being required. Also, if the business is sold each owner would pay tax on the capital gains based on the tax bracket they are currently in. Another possible reason for doing this is to spread some of the income being generated by the business to others, who may be taxed at a lower rate. I'm not sure of this client's reasoning for the amendment, but he did not notify the bank that he was contemplating such a change, nor did he notify them after it was completed. His business account continued to operate as it always had. At a later date he made a request to increase his business line of credit to assist with an equipment purchase. At the time of the request it was the bank's requirement that all persons owning 10% or more of the company had to sign for the business loan. As the two children owned more than 10% each and were underage, they could not sign, therefore the loan request was declined—not because the business owner didn't qualify for the loan but because of the change in ownership of the business.

In the event of the death of one partner in an incorporated company, the business account can continue to operate as long as the signing authority requirements can still be met. In other words, if the account documents say "any one of the owners" can sign on behalf of the business and there are other owners remaining, then the account can continue to operate.

IMPORTANT NOTE:

Be sure you understand the purpose and effect of signing a personal guarantee before putting your signature on one for any business transaction.

Personal guarantees can be "unlimited" for the full amount of the debt or "limited" to a specific dollar amount. It may be necessary to sign one if you require business credit, however, you should still understand what the consequences could be if the business fails. Banks or other companies you deal with may require the guarantee as additional security for granting credit should your company fail to repay the debt. Normally a reasonable amount of time is given and several attempts are made to get the business to pay. Only after the efforts to collect have been exhausted would the debtor make a claim against the guarantee that you signed. A personal guarantee document is enforceable in court. It really can mean you will have to come up with the money to repay the business debt personally. I am aware of a couple of small business owners who did not manage their credit very wisely and had to sell their homes to cover their financial irresponsibility.

A personal guarantee is a promise to repay a debt yourself, should someone else not be able to. Occasionally, when young adults are first borrowing for a car or their university education they have no "track record" to confirm that they are responsible persons and are capable of repaying such a debt. It may be that their loan application could be declined unless their parents are willing to guarantee that the loan will be repaid should their child default. Once the child has established their own credit worthiness, such a guarantee will no longer be required. When it comes to an incorporated company, you will remember that legally this type of business is considered an individual and the company owners are not responsible for any of the business debts. The same premise above applies: until the company has developed its own satisfactory track record for debt repayment, it may be required that the business owners pledge their personal guarantee. Should the company fail to pay the debt they will become personally responsible. In other words if the company has no money to cover the monthly loan payment or any assets to sell to repay a delinquent loan in full, the owners will have to look into their own pockets.

My Business Issues and Plans:

2.

Setting Up Your Business Accounts: What You Should Know About Business Banking

What you don't want to happen

Brad and Marty, two young men in their late 20s, owned and managed a very profitable gardening business as a partnership for two years. Their business strengths complemented each other and they got along very well. Brad concentrated on managing the work crew. Marty was in charge of the office and business development. During the second year of the partnership Brad divorced his wife and began a new relationship. Brad was short of money because of his divorce and decided it would be alright to set up his new residence using funds from the business operating line of credit. Some $20,000 later, Marty became aware that the extra cash had been drawn from the bank account. He came into my bank to request they stop paying cheques that were being written by Brad for his new apartment, but continue to allow other genuine business cheques to be paid. Since only one of the two partners was required to sign cheques, the bank could not comply with the request. The issue was between the two business owners and they needed to settle the problem themselves.

While a business account and credit line should only be

used for business purposes, a bank cannot monitor and judge which cheques are rightfully being written against the account and which might not be. If the bank becomes aware of this type of problem it may result in the restriction of many or all business bank account services. In extreme cases, if the issue is not resolved, the partners could receive a request to pay out the credit line and close their account.

In the end, because personal guarantees had been signed for the business credit line, both partners were jointly responsible to repay the business loan in full, including the additional funds that were withdrawn by the one partner. Neither of them had a clear understanding of their individual personal responsibility for the business' financial obligations when they began their partnership. Unfortunately, they also did not have a legal partnership agreement and could not resolve their differences. The dispute effectively closed down what had previously been a very successful business.

What you do want to happen

Roger was a partner in a fairly large family business. The Roberts Company manufactured and shipped water quality equipment all over the world. Roger had worked in the business for over ten years and was responsible for managing the business bank accounts and preparing internal financial reports. As part of his duties, Roger regularly faxed the bank with wire payment instructions to cover the cost of manufacturing materials that were purchased. His bank was well aware of these normal business transactions.

One day the bank received a new fax. It was on the standard company business fax letterhead and had Roger's signature as usual. However, the fax was requesting $50,000 in funds be sent to Japan. While the Roberts Company sent many wire payments, it was not normal for the payments to be sent out of the country. In addition, the amount of the funds being transferred was usually less than $30,000. Even though the signature and letterhead looked fine, the bank called Roger to verify the instructions as per their fax validation protocol. It wasn't real. Someone had gotten a copy of the company letterhead and bank information along with Roger's signature. They were trying to scam money from the business account. Thanks to his bank's fax validation procedures the funds never left the bank account.

It's been my experience that businesses that have a good working relationship with their bank may be paying smaller service charges, use banking products that suit their specific needs, and have few if any banking problems. But that's not because they get special favours! The more you keep in touch with your bank account manager and discuss your business financial issues and challenges with them the more they can ensure you have the right account and the best type of services to help your finances run smoothly. The more you get to know them the more they will get to know you. If you only call after you have a problem, you have limited what they can do for you—if they can do anything at all. Don't expect to just drop into your local corner branch and find the expertise you need. While there are many top quality small business bankers and advisors to be found in Canadian banks, they may be located in specific branches. Be sure to spend some time to find one that has the training and expertise that you need to help you understand your banking options.

TYPES OF BANK ACCOUNTS
Sole ownership business accounts

Only you can be a signatory on this account type. That's what a sole ownership is all about, it's only you. If you really need someone else to assist you with your business banking you can designate someone as your power of attorney. If you allow a POA on your account they can sign for any withdrawal and have access to any business account information. They would not be able to make any account changes or apply for a business loan in the business' name. Nevertheless, you should be very cautious to whom you grant this access. Any transaction on the account that are completed by a POA would be your sole responsibility. You should note that a power of attorney ceases on death, therefore a POA will not be allowed access to your account if you should die.

Partnership business accounts

A partnership can have two, three, or more partners—so how you set up your business account is important. As a partner you will always have access to information about the account such as the balance and a listing of cheques paid; however, unless you are actually designated as a signatory, you will not be able to sign cheques. The partners need to decide who will be in control of the account, who will manage the cash and cheques for deposit, and who will handle the bills and cheques written. This can mean everyone has access to the account (which could be a bookkeeping nightmare) or only one person. As noted previously, no matter which partner has signing authority on the account, all general partners are legally responsible for the bank account's operation.

Will you also need access for any non-partners or employees? Will the bookkeeper or the secretary need to make deposits, buy money orders, or pick up coin orders? Be sure you discuss these requirements with your banker, since limited access can be provided for these purposes. The bank can advise how you can restrict access to your account to only what is necessary for your staff.

You should make sure your business bank statement is

sent directly to you (or another partner) and that you verify it monthly, even if someone else is doing your bookkeeping. Having access to the business account balance and transactions over the Internet is also considered both safe and advisable. See also "Safeguarding Your Assets" for further general banking information.

Corporate business accounts

Corporations generally have the same concerns as a partnership account and should follow the general information noted above.

Larger businesses also usually have more complex banking requirements. Establishing an open communication with your banker would be beneficial. The more they know about you and your business, the more financial advice can be provided and services recommended. Some specific options for larger businesses:

Cash management

Payroll Services—someone else keeps up to date with all the taxation rules, pays all staff, remits source deductions, and sends you the year end T4 tax slips.

Deposit Acceleration or Transfer Services—for use when the business operates several accounts and needs to move money frequently between them. This can help maximize interest that is being earned or save on borrowing costs.

Pre-authorized Payments—automatic withdrawals from clients' accounts to collect your monthly billing from them.

Direct Deposit—payment is deposited directly into bank account instead of writing cheques

Government Tax Payment and Filing—management of your weekly, monthly, or quarterly tax payments (payroll deductions, corporate tax, personal tax, federal and provincial taxes, etc.). You provide the tax information amounts and dates and a third party ensures that the taxes are paid on time when due. The filings are done electronically, eliminating your requirement to manually complete the tax forms and remit a cheque for payment. This also ensures you never pay a late filing fee.

Account Receivable Management—where your clients provide their approval for EFT (electronic funds transfer) withdrawals from their account to pay your bill. You get paid automatically, on time, every month. There is the added potential to reduce your in house billing administrative costs.

Trade finance

Import/Export Letters of Credit—these are guarantees obtained through your bank. For importing, the letter guarantees that the business sending you supplies or products will get paid as soon as you pick them up. The supplier will "draw" on the letter of credit through your bank's head office. The head office debits your branch for payment. (You need to qualify for these just as you would a loan.) On the flip side if you send an export shipment to someone else you can request they provide you with a letter of credit to guarantee that you will be paid. These are usually used for larger dollar transactions and especially for international shipments.

Standby Letters of Credit—this type of letter of credit is not just for one transaction as the above are. They are used as a type of last resort for unpaid debts. For instance, the Ontario Lottery and Gaming Corporation requires convenience stores to provide them with a standby letter of credit in order to sell lottery tickets. As long as you make you payments to them as required it is not used, but if you do not pay them they will removed you from their sellers list and call on the bank's head office to pay your debt to them in full. Again, the bank will debit your branch to collect the funds so you must be pre-qualified to obtain a standby letter of credit.

Documentary Collections—also a service for importing or exporting goods. In this instance you do not need to pre-qualify for a letter of credit or pay in advance for the shipment. When the international shipment is sent, collection documents are also sent to your bank at the same time. You will have an opportunity to inspect the shipment but not to pick it up. If everything is as you expected you then arrange for payment to be made through your bank. Once payment is completed the documents are released to you in order for the goods to be cleared through customs and released.

Merchant services

Credit and Debit Card Processing—the system you require to be able to accept credit and debit card transactions

Foreign exchange services

Direct Online Trading—for those businesses that have a high level of importing and/or exporting and often need to exchange large amounts of foreign currencies. There is the opportunity to buy at a discount rate and save conversion costs.

Specialized business services

Franchising—if you are buying into a franchise business (Tim Hortons, Quiznos Subs, Second Cup, Pizza Pizza) different banks will have specialized financing and banking packages available for those who qualify.

Agriculture—specialized lending/banking suited specifically to the agricultural industry.

Professionals (accountant, dentist, lawyer, etc.)—specialized lending/banking geared towards services professionals need from a bank.

Aboriginal—specialized services that reflect aboriginal banking needs.

All of these services can be helpful financial tools and are available at most banks. Moving these types of duties to qualified external providers can be a sound risk management choice. Shifting some of the accounting and banking out of your office to an outside professional organization will reduce the chances of fraud happening. It is also possible that with their specifically focused expertise you may save a few dollars, not to mention the time savings for you or your staff. I'm not saying these extras are needed by every business but, depending on your situation, they may be well worth the cost.

GENERAL SMALL BUSINESS BANKING INFORMATION

Canada's Anti-Money Laundering and Anti-Terrorist Financing Initiative (FINTRAC)

FINTRAC was created in July 2000 to be Canada's anti-money laundering "financial intelligence unit" that captures, records, analyses, and traces suspected money laundering and terrorist activities. When warranted, information gathered is supplied to Canadian and international police agencies to assist with fraud or terrorism investigations and prosecutions.

The following types of institutions are required to participate in specific data collection (required from both businesses and individuals):

- accountants
- casinos
- financial service companies
- money service businesses
- securities dealers
- real estate brokers, sales agents, or developers

- life insurance dealers
- British Columbia notaries
- legal counsel and legal firms
- dealers in precious metals and stones

If you are a business owner engaged in these activities and you receive or pay out monies (other than your normal fees) or you purchase and sell specific types of goods for others, you will be required by law to keep detailed records of the identity of the parties with which you have completed the transactions. The information required includes the person's name, address, and details of valid identity documents (driver's licence, birth certificate, credit cards, etc.) including noting where the funds came from (by cheque, money order, or cash). You are required to record and report all large cash transactions (over $10,000) that you process for any of your clients. Additionally, you must report any other transactions that you suspect may be money laundering—no matter the dollar value.

Administrative penalties or fines can be levied against a business operation for non-compliance. Criminal penalties for failing to collect and maintain proper documentation for these transactions range from $500,000 to $2,000,000 for a first offence and can include up to five years imprisonment.

For further information specifically related to each of these lines of business, refer to the FINTRAC website: *www.fintrac.gc.ca*

Proceeds of Crime (Money Laundering) and Terrorist Financing Act (PCMLTFA)

PCMLTFA covers the following legislation:

The Proceeds of Crime (Money Laundering) and Terrorist Financing Suspicious Transaction Reporting Regulations

- details what information must be recorded in a suspicious transaction report
- determines the time frame and the report outline
- determines what information FINTRAC can release

The Proceeds of Crime (Money Laundering) and Terrorist Financing Regulations

- determines customer identification and record keeping requirements
- determines what type of transactions need to be reported and the time frame for reporting

The Cross-Border Currency and Monetary Instruments Reporting Regulations

- provides a definition of "monetary" instruments
- determines the reporting limit and time line for report submissions

The Proceeds of Crime (Money Laundering) and Terrorist Financing Registration Regulations

- provides additional information for registration purposes

The Proceeds of Crime (Money Laundering) and Terrorist-Financing Administrative Monetary Penalties Regulations

- sets out specific violations and their classifications

The above legislations ensure that all banks and financial institutions have identification requirements in place that must be satisfied before anyone can open and transact business on a bank account. Each financial institution may have their own specific requirements, however, usually all business partners with between 10–25% ownership or more need to be present and have two pieces of valid identification (one piece of picture ID is mandatory) to open an account. Special requirements can usually be made for any non-resident business partners, which will require a solicitor in their country of residence. In addition to the two pieces of identification account holders are also required to provide the following information:

- name
- address
- date of birth
- occupation

If the account will be operated on behalf of a third party, all of the above information is also required for that person.

If you are starting up a new business you may find that "access to funds" within your business account may initially be restricted. Access to funds is related to your bank's "hold funds" policy. It may mean that after you deposit a cheque into your account, you may not be able to withdraw any funds until a specific period of time has elapsed. This holding period is to allow time to confirm whether the cheque you deposited has "cleared" the bank account it was written on. In most cases one week is usually sufficient to determine if a cheque will be returned to the bank "non-sufficient funds" (NSF). Unfortunately, it can take much longer than one week for a cheque to be returned if it is fraudulent. In any event, you need to be aware whenever the bank releases the funds payment of the cheque remains your complete responsibility. In other words, if you withdraw the money and the cheque is later returned NSF, or as a forgery, you are entirely responsible to repay the bank in full. If you have restricted access to your funds, once your business has been operating satisfactorily for a reasonable period of time, your access to funds limit can usually be reassessed.

You should note that the above reference to cheques being deposited might also include bank drafts and money orders in addition to personal cheques. When I began my bank career several years ago, bank drafts and money orders were considered guaranteed funds; they were seldom found to be counterfeit. Today these types of payments are very frequently forged and as such the same cheque clearing time periods may also be in place for these items. Asking your clients to provide you with a money order instead of a personal cheque will unfortunately no longer prevent your business from being defrauded.

Monthly business account statements should always be mailed to and received by the business owner and not a bookkeeper or employee. Banks usually require you to review the statement and notify them of any irregularities within 30 days. I would suggest that, as an owner, you personally verify that the statement is correct. If you have a very active account it might be beneficial if your transactions were reviewed more often via online banking. Canadian cheque clearing rules state that an NSF cheque must be returned to the cashing bank within 48 hours of being presented for payment. A forged cheque (where the cheque date, payee, amount, or account owner's signature is altered) can take 60-90 days to be returned. It's up to you to advise your bank as soon as possible if a fraudulent cheque was paid on your account. If these deadlines are passed, the cashing bank does not have to accept the return of the cheque. Note that cheques cashed with a forged endorsement (the person who signed the back of the cheque is not the real person who it is payable to) have a return period of six years. Refer to the Canadian Payments Association links under "References" for additional information.

Returned cheques actually cost your business much more than the $35–60 NSF fee. Having even a couple of them may affect your business account history and your borrowing ability.

NOTE: For business accounts, not only do you pay a fee for any cheques that you write that are NSF, you will also pay a fee if any of the client cheques you deposit are returned NSF.

If you are opening a new business bank account and therefore have no business banking track record, it is possible you may not be immediately allowed access to your account through the Automated Bank Machine (ABM) system. You may also not yet qualify for overdraft protection or a business line of credit. An existing satisfactory personal banking record may substitute for the lack of a business track record, but not necessarily. New businesses have inherent risks that owners are not always aware of, such as managing the risks of accepting bad cheques or payments from clients you do not really know. You should be aware as well that in addition to the possibility of cheques being returned NSF it is also possible for credit card payments to be debited back to your account if the transaction is disputed by the cardholder. You need to know who your customers are if you will be accepting cheques or credit card payments from them. It usually takes time for a new business owner to gain insight into the type of clients they attract and what payment methods work best for them. Once you have established a satisfactory business banking record, additional services may become available to you. Internet access to view your account balance and activities should be available immediately.

While it has become quite routine for individuals to have the ability to complete banking transactions at different branches across the country or use the ABMs of other financial institutions, business account dealings can be more restrictive. You should have a thorough discussion with your bank representative as to where, when, and how you can operate the account. Questions to ask include:

- Can you make deposits only at the branch the account was opened at or can this be done at other locations?
- Can you cash cheques or make withdrawals at other locations? What about purchasing a money order? Or getting an account balance?
- Can you use the services of another bank to access your business account?

If you operate your business at several locations or are on the road often you may find that you require access for one or more alternate branches to cover your banking needs. This would be the ability to bank in branch in addition to having other ABM or Internet accesses granted. If this is the case, you may be required to make pre-approved special arrangements.

Will you or other company officers have a bank identification card for the business? If you receive one be sure to use it when you complete any bank transactions. The card is used not only for ABM and Internet access, but also to identify you as a client at the Customer Service Representative's wicket. If you have provided one of your employees a bank transaction card for the business account, it will be programmed for only the activities that they are allowed to do for you. They should only be using the specific card that was meant for them and never borrowing someone else's. When the card is used the bank will be able to determine, at a later date, whose card was used and when. If you have several persons transacting business on your behalf, this information may assist you should you ever have any questions about your account activity. Presenting the card in the branch will also help ensure that there are no mistakes or transaction errors made on your account. (Unfortunately, this does happen occasionally—we are all human.)

Ask questions about how your bank deals with telephone requests, communications by fax, and whether email contact is allowed. Banks will have restrictions on these activities in order to ensure that they are dealing with you and not someone pretending to be you. You should be aware of what processes the bank has put in place to ensure they are receiving legitimate requests for your account. These extra precautions may slightly delay some transactions or necessitate further investigation. I think this is an excellent protection mechanism for your account, though some bank clients feel it is a service inconvenience.

CHEQUE SCAMS

Cheque scams were one of the earliest types of fraud. Even though today we embrace ATMs and electronic banking of all sorts, billions of cheque payments continue to be made every year, in Canada and in many other countries worldwide. Due to the significantly large volume of cheques being passed, this type of transaction remains the primary business enterprise of many con artists.

The Canadian Payments Association Statistics for 2008

Percentage of Paper Versus Electronic Items Flowing Through the Automated Clearing Settlement System (ACSS) for 2008

	Paper	Electronic
Volume	17.92%	82.08%
Value	61.35%	38.65%

(www.cdnpay.ca/publications/acss_percent.asp)

Flow of Payment Items Through the Automated Clearing Settlement System (ACSS) for 2008

Small Cheques <$50,000

Volume: 997,146,998
Value*:   1,136,126,100

Large Cheques >$50,000

Volume: 7,886,482
Value*:   2,057,549,746

*($000 CDN)

(www.cdnpay.ca/publications/acss_q99.asp)

Cheque fraud situations include:

- real customers who pass bad cheques on their own accounts (where they are perfectly aware that there are no funds in the account to cover the cheque)
- persons who pass cheques written on genuine accounts (whether open or since closed) where they pretend to be the owner of the account and where there may or may not be sufficient funds in the account to cover the cheque
- other persons who attempt to pass cheques drawn on completely make believe accounts

Cheque fraud also includes persons who do not claim to be the owner or writer of the cheque but state that the cheque (often purported to be a "payroll" cheque) is legitimate and is rightfully payable to them. These persons usually attempt to cash the fraudulent cheques through a bank. They might also approach a store and request that the cheque be cashed or exchanged for merchandise. In most of these cases the individuals in possession of the cheques are well aware that they are fraudulent. They are usually payable to someone (real or fictitious) for whom they have acquired fake ID. There are also a few unsuspecting bank clients who occasionally wish to cash or deposit these types of cheques, accepted in payment for some service or sale, who are unaware of the cheque scam being perpetrated against them.

How can you protect yourself from fraud for items drawn on your account?

- Ensure the business account you open either returns your original cheques or provides a copy of each item that is paid through your account and review each one when you receive your monthly statement

- Use electronic or pre-authorized payments when available
- Use envelopes that cannot be seen though when mailing cheques
- Keep blank cheques in a secure location
- Destroy cheques from closed accounts
- Reconcile your statement as soon as you receive it
- Use continuous serial numbers when ordering cheques
- Have only one set of cheques for each account
- Use high quality cheques with security features
- Report any outstanding cheques and account frauds immediately

I have noted many behaviours above that will help ensure your business name and bank account will not be used by fraudsters to create these counterfeit cheques. It is never a onetime thing. Once an account is compromised, hundreds and perhaps thousands of cheques might be printed and put in circulation. The more there are, the higher the chance one of them will get cashed. There are also several ways to support your business and staff in avoiding accepting these bad cheques. In Chapter 6, "Know Who Your Clients Are," refer to the section "Accepting Personal Cheques" (page 112) for specific details.

In any event, if you do get caught in a cheque fraud scam be sure to alert your bank and to also contact the police to report the incident. The best opportunity to recover any lost funds is if the incident is discovered and reported quickly. Unfortunately, in most cases, there is little chance that you will be able to recoup what was stolen from you. What's that famous quote? Your best defence is a good offence.

My Business Issues and Plans:

3.

Setting Up Your Office and Warehouse: Safeguarding Your Assets

What you don't want to happen

Paul and his brother Sam had been running their father's business since he retired five years earlier. It was a mid-sized distribution company with a fleet of transport trucks that were on the road every day. Late one evening, one of the drivers had a tractor-trailer unit stolen when he was stopped mid-route at a roadside restaurant for dinner. There had been a rash of brazen transport cargo thefts on this particular major highway corridor over the previous six months, but the theft still caught the business by surprise. One week later, the trailer was found abandoned with all of the shipment missing. The truck cab was never seen again.

The situation caused several problems for the transport business. While they did have insurance liability coverage, it ended up taking six weeks for the cargo loss to be processed and repaid by the insurer. In the meantime, the client chose to switch to another trucking company that they considered more secure. The stolen truck cab was also eventually replaced and the trailer put back on the road. In the end, the business lost one of its best clients and several smaller ones due to the incident. It also lost a number of weeks' sales due to the trailer not being on the road. It took seven months to replace the lost clients. Even though insurance covered the majority of the price tag for the thefts, their net income short-fall for the year was $106,000.

What you do want to happen

What if the business above had had a GPS system installed in both the tractor and trailer? The thieves might have quickly been located by police and the tractor-trailer and cargo could have been recovered without loss or damage. It's not a farfetched solution anymore. GPS trackers are now being added to most high-priced construction equipment. Expensive cars now also routinely have them installed. The cost of the GPS system (approximately $1,000) or a vehicle immobilizer would have been well worth the early recovery of a tractor-trailer loaded with cargo—both in terms of the financial price tag of having one less transport vehicle on the road, as well as the theft insurance claim for the unit, not to mention the issue of dealing with the missing client cargo.

In one actual case, an excavation company that operated heavy equipment had a bulldozer stolen from a work site. It wasn't even one month old when it was taken and it had come equipped with a GPS system. As soon as the equipment moved off site the construction supervisor was notified and police were called. The unit was located within a few hours, actually parked in the thief's driveway!

Securing assets should be a central concern for all small businesses. Assets obviously include your inventory and equipment, but it is really much more than this. Information of all types is also a business asset, starting with "personal" information about the business itself, such as banking information, owner signatures, and the list of all your suppliers. You will also likely hold client records with various pieces of their personal information—including bank or credit card info. What about your employees? Social insurance and health card numbers, addresses, and dates of birth are normally held in personnel files. All of this information is just as important as any other business property.

In February 2008, the RCMP in British Columbia busted an ID theft ring. In the basement of a house they found Canada Post uniforms, 2,400 stolen pieces of mail, and credit card making equipment. They also seized more than 100 CDs full of stolen personal information. One CD alone had private and confidential information for 3,000 people. Another CD held the data for another 20,000. The information they had gleaned consisted of names, addresses, dates of birth, social insurance numbers, employment, and salary, plus the names of their spouses and children. The thieves were suspected of obtaining all of the information from business and home mailboxes after the mail delivery was completed. They had enough equipment and materials to manufacture fake credit and debit cards, driver's licences, passports, and medical insurance cards. Also found was an apparatus that assisted in tracing signatures. They had authentic tax returns, credit cards, and government, personal, and business cheques. In other words, if any of this information belonged to you, you would not know what hit you when the credit cards bills and collection agency calls started coming in. The amount of information and equipment seized was considered a mid-level haul. Two people were indicted with various fraud and impersonation charges.

Some things to consider to ensure all your business assets are kept safe:

OFFICE SECURITY

I will assume your business is very important to you—your inventory, your equipment, and your clients. Wherever you keep these items (or information about them)—whether

in a warehouse, an office, or the basement of your home—
they should be protected. Be attentive when giving service
people access to your place of business. For instance, it's not
a good idea to leave your filing cabinets with private client
information unlocked overnight when the janitor is coming
in. Likewise, leaving the plumber alone in the warehouse
while you go on a sales call may also not be a good idea. I
think most employees are honest, but unfortunately a few are
not. Allow access to your building or client files only to those
who need to have it, and keep track of who you have given
permission to enter. Ensure they know that they can't share
their key or password with anyone else. You don't have to
duplicate Fort Knox, just determine what is important to you
and set up internal guidelines that are always followed. I can
tell you that the unremarkable theft of a box of your company
letterhead along with a sample copy of the boss's signature
could spell future trouble.

Be on the alert for overly friendly people who seem to
hang around your sales area or staff frequently. Sometimes
these people may be "casing" out your business for a future
theft. They are trying to find out as much as they can about
what you may have on site or in your offices that can be
stolen. The more they hang around, the more people talk to
them, and the more they learn. They could also be trying to
gain your or an employee's confidence for a different reason.
They want you to become very familiar with them and develop a level of trust. In the end they may try to use this trust
to perpetrate some type of scam.

Cheques for your business account (and personal accounts for that matter) should not be accessible to anyone
who does not have signing authority. In fact, when a business
cheque is used it would be sensible for the cheque ledger to
be updated right away. If an error is made and a cheque is ru-

ined the ledger should reflect that. You could also keep a copy of the bungled cheque attached to the ledger book page to ensure no one has gone home with it. Missing blank cheques should be investigated—a stop payment can be lodged at the bank if you believe one has gone astray. When ordering new cheques you should pay particular attention to the cheque serial numbers. A cheque book serial number would start with the number 1 and go to 100 or 200. When you reorder you should start the new cheque order with the next number in line—101 or 201. Using the cheques in sequential order will assist you in noticing if any have gone missing. Order cheques only through a reputable supplier and only order as many as you need. Don't order a large supply that will last you a few years. If you do, you may not notice any cheques gone missing for several months.

If you have a rural mailbox or one that may be accessible to others, find out the general time mail delivery takes place and make sure to pick it up as soon as possible. Never put out mail for pickup in a rural box—drive to town and mail it at a post office. Rural mail and postal boxes are often vandalized both to steal the cheques you have written to others and for any business or personal information that can be used in a fraud or scam. This type of theft has been happening for years, and is still prevalent today. It might also be wise to have a protocol in the office with respect to mail. If there is someone in particular who is responsible for incoming and outgoing mail it is less likely to be lost. You might consider couriers or registered mail for important correspondence or shipments.

While I do not have any specific statistics to suggest mailbox pilfering is on the rise, I do know that identity theft remains a sizeable problem. I have read some RCMP divisional warnings posted during 2007–2009 concerning large scale mail theft that happened in specific Canadian locations. Further, news articles over the past few years have noted several fraud rings busted by police were found to have significant amounts of stolen mail along with the usual counterfeit cheques, ID, and credit cards.

Do you know what a fraudulent money order, bank draft, or cheque looks like? How about cash? There is certainly counterfeit money in circulation these days. If you do know how to identify fraudulent money or cheques, how about your staff? Have you trained them in how to recognize a potentially fraudulent transaction? For further information and tips on this topic, see Chapter 6.

FIRE SAFETY

What about the safety and security of your people? Do you have office rules regarding fires or other emergencies? How about emergency contact numbers for staff? It would be a good idea to have something spelled out and posted in the office along with a basic first aid kit.

Your business premises may be subject to provincial fire and safety regulations—you need to find out from your municipality if any of these rules apply to you. Be aware that failure to comply with municipal safety laws can subject you and your business to fines. A business in my area was recently fined $3,000 for not having a safety plan or fire extinguishers in a rental apartment building.

How do you determine if your office is at risk for a fire or accident? Review the following issues:

- Are office desks, walkways, or storage rooms packed to the ceiling or cluttered with debris?
- Are emergency exits clearly marked and is access unimpeded by furniture or other objects? Are those exit doors locked?

- Do you have the proper number of fire extinguishers and is their charge checked annually? Do employees know where they are and how to use them?
- Do you have a first aid kit? Do employees know where it is?
- Do you have a water sprinkler system? Has it been tested lately?
- Are there cover plates on all electrical outlets? How many items are plugged into them?
- Is your electrical panel in good order? Is the electrical room full of junk or the panel blocked by packages?
- Is your office building number posted on the outside of the building and visible from the roadway for emergency vehicles to see?
- Do you have any hazardous materials in the office or warehouse? Are they properly labelled and stored?
- Are gas or other fuel lines properly marked?
- Do staff have a plan to follow in case of a fire or emergency? Is it reviewed? If so, how often?

INSURANCE COVERAGE

Make sure that you explore all of the different types of insurance available to your business. Here is some basic business insurance coverage that is available:

1. Fire—this should include buildings that you own and office equipment/furniture and records. You can add coverage here for storms, flooding, and vandalism, etc.
2. Liability—coverage for accidents to persons or non-owned vehicles/equipment
3. Automobile/vehicle—whether licensed for the road or for use on-site
4. Business interruption—coverage for loss of income if the business cannot operate for a period of time due to circumstances beyond your control (i.e., fire)

5. Crime—burglary, robbery, theft (by employees or others), etc.
6. Rent—if you are renting your business premises and need to move temporarily in case of fire or other problems

WAREHOUSE OR INVENTORY SECURITY

Inventory can be anything, from large garden-ready piles of dirt to expensive jewellery or inexpensive cans of tomato sauce. What type of inventory will your business require to operate? How much of it will you need to have on hand at any one time? What would the value of this inventory be? In addition to making sure you have insurance against fire and theft, you should determine whether additional security measures are warranted. You may be surprised to know that at garden centres, theft of large quantities of plain ordinary dirt is not unknown. Regardless of the type of inventory, theft is costly to all businesses.

Locks, gates, safes, security cameras, and pass card access are a few things to think about for inventory protection. Which you chose will depend on the size and value of the items and the costs of putting the protection in place.

Locks and gates are not necessarily just for main doors or entrances. You might consider what else is in your business premises that you'd like to protect or restrict access to.

How about the electrical room? Why? That might be where your computer mainframe or server is located. There would really be no need for anyone other than a qualified service person to have access to this room.

Do you have a filing room? If your business maintains a significant number of private client records, even if the individual cabinets are locked, a secure room would mean the information is doubly protected. Only those who have a reason to use the files should have access to the room.

A safe would be advisable if the business handles any amount of money or cheques (other than a few dollars in petty cash). A small cash till is very portable and certainly easier to steal than a heavy safe. A safe is also more secure if it requires two individuals to access it.

If you wish to use security cameras, you will need to determine what it is you'd like to observe and document. Do you want a record of all clients entering the driveway and parking lot? The building itself? Or, just the ones in a particular area of the store where more thefts occur? Perhaps you just want to be able to see who is in the work area or outdoor yard and what activities are going on? Or only to record client sales transactions? You will need to be prepared to maintain and service the units or have another company do so on your behalf. Will this be additional private data that you will need to store? Will the tapes be erased periodically and if so when? Newer cameras now store the pictures on a computer hard drive (with capacity limitations).

A competent security service can review your business needs and expand on your many options here.

All inventory holdings should be managed with a tracking record whether on paper (if you must) or computer based (first choice). Someone needs to be accountable for updating the records for everything that enters or leaves the warehouse or store. There should be more than one person equally responsible for verifying the information. It is a normal procedure to complete a full inventory count once each year for tax purposes. If possible, you should schedule inventory verification more often than that. Inventory tracking is not only for the items you are selling, but also for any equipment that you use to operate the business. For instance, you should maintain a running list of all computer equipment along with serial numbers. Then there are printers, fax machines, cash registers, adding machines, trucks, vans, and tools. The list can be used for tax purposes and theft or fire insurance claims.

Any warehouse or larger retail business can consider anti-theft security devices and tags or actual security guards if warranted. RFID tag information is covered in Chapter 10.

You will not likely be surprised to know that if you purchase any supplies off the back of a truck that just happened to be in your neighbourhood you could either be purchasing inferior products or stolen goods. Some thieves literally sell their stolen wares from the backs of cars, vans, and trucks. I read of the theft of a few hundred packages of frozen meat from a warehouse. The crook was caught when he went door to door in a neighbouring town saying he had just made a delivery to a local supermarket but had brought too much product with him. He didn't want to haul it all back to storage—he was willing to sell it all at a *significant discount* to save himself the trip back! Another potential fraud could happen when a person knocks on your door and tells you they just "re-sealed" the driveway of a neighbour and want to know if you would like yours done too? Since they are already on the street and they have left over sealant it would be a really great price. Under this circumstance there's a good chance that they are not a valid business and are probably using inferior products.

There are many other ideas that you might consider that would assist you in protecting your business assets. If you carry large or expensive inventory holdings or have a special risk issue, I encourage you to discuss your situation with an established colleague or a protection specialist in your line of business.

COMPUTER SECURITY

Computer information protection should be a high priority for any business. Just as important as the software you will purchase to manage your company, your Internet security firewalls and password access protocols, and regular data backup requirements should be a vital part of your computer operating system. If you maintain proprietary business information and personal client records on a computer's hard drives, you should ensure that your staff has access only to the files they need to see to complete their work. Employees have been known to make copies of confidential information that is then sold to identity theft scammers.

Electronic messages have the potential to pose problems. Email passes though many different routers and servers before it arrives at the receiving person. Along the way there is always the possibility that the email can be intercepted. There are sophisticated data mining programs now available that have the ability to obtain email copies that have been backed up on outside servers. If you are using email for general correspondence or exchange of public information this should not pose a problem. If you are, however, sending sensitive information via email, encryption should be used—especially if you or your staff will be using laptops. Laptop users should also be careful when using wireless local area network (WLAN) hotspot services. You need to understand that when you use such a service, the WLAN host provider may have a program that allows him complete access to your laptop files if they are not password security protected. Beware of anyone offering "free" WLAN services—this may be their plan! These types of WLAN issues also work in reverse if you offer the service in your business office to staff. If the system is not password protected, others nearby, even outside your building, may also be able to access your network and therefore your computer files, too. People who tap into your wireless system may just be looking for free Internet access, but some know how to use WLAN to access your own computer system and files. Others have been known to use wireless access for illegal purposes, such as downloading movies or music. In this case, the affected companies would be able to trace the illegal activity back to you.

Your employees should also be aware that, by law, business computers are workplace equipment and their supervisor has every right to monitor their use. An email sent from a company PC is considered the property of the business and can be searched for and read at any time by management. If you have a reason to keep close tabs on your employee's computer use you can install software surveillance to monitor email, keystrokes, websites visited, and file access, which can automatically be mailed to your own address hourly or daily, including screenshots. If you resort to this type of activity, I would caution that the employees must be notified that such monitoring is being done regularly.

Servicing of computer equipment should always be completed by a reliable company if you value the information that you have stored there. If you travel with a laptop or if it is being transported for repair it should be done securely. Computers should never be left unattended or in an unlocked vehicle. You may remember recent newspaper reports of a couple of laptops and hard drives that went missing in transit with thousands of private client files and credit card numbers on them. Your laptop may be protected by a password, but I assure you it won't take long for a professional to crack it. I'm also sure you wouldn't want to have to deal with the theft of your client's (or your business') confidential information.

Not to be forgotten, be sure also to keep a boot up password and regularly change passwords to keep unwanted eyes out. There is always a risk to the security of your company data if your employees are using their work computer to visit non-business websites, especially if they are downloading anything off an unknown site. Sometimes malware will request installation agreements, or may employ trickery to gain privileges on the computer. Malware is a computer term used to denote all types of hostile computer programs which are developed to surreptitiously gain access to computers without the system owner's consent. Some malware is merely of an annoying prankish nature while others have a more malicious intent. Pop-ups may promote a product as a solution to a non-existent problem. For example, a website may claim to "scan your hard disc" as you web surf, but this is actually infeasible and should only be pre-empted with a pop-up blocker. Employees loading or directly accessing computer files from home can also have computer viruses or worms that will transfer an infection to a business computer. Any malicious software could cause slowing of system resources, crashes, lost data, and irreparable harm to your hardware. Simply connecting to the Internet you will encounter attempts to access your computer externally within five minutes! If someone gains access to confidential information, your business reputation may be irreparably damaged.

BUSINESS AND CLIENT INFORMATION SECURITY

I've been talking about computer and laptop protection, but there is another simple way you can ensure the security of your data.

In addition to computer and filing cabinet security measures, you should make certain that all paper garbage that may contain client information is shredded daily rather than being placed directly in recycling bins or in garbage bags for thieves to find. For some, dumpster diving is a lucrative new calling. Personal client information is stolen and sold at an alarming rate these days. Putting some key controls in place will help make sure the theft of personal information won't happen to your business.

In the normal course of business, quite a lot of personal information can be collected from clients, such as names, addresses, and credit card numbers. In some cases you may have reason to collect much more private information: Health Card numbers (massage therapy), insurance policy information (auto repairs), or Social Insurance Numbers (tax accountants). You should collect and keep only information you need to know about your clients and nothing more.

Personal Information Protection and Electronic Documents Act **(PIPEDA)**

The *Personal Information Protection and Electronic Documents Act* (PIPEDA) came into effect beginning in 2001. From the Office of the Privacy Commissioner of Canada, it is a regulatory requirement that businesses must follow to ensure protection of personal information.

PIPEDA states that when you obtain personal information from clients you must first explain why you need the information and what you intend to do with it. For some types of information you will need their explicit consent (in writing), such as to obtain a copy of their Credit Bureau report. If you will be providing any of their information to a third party this must also be disclosed. You many only hold this information as long as it is required for the purpose that it was obtained. If you no longer need it, it must be destroyed or deleted.

PIPEDA also states that all employees are required to know and understand the business privacy protection policies and procedures. They must be able to discuss the regulations with clients including being able to advise them of how and to whom they can file a complaint against your company.

What is considered personal information?

Name, address, age, identification, ethnicity, correspondence, comments, assessments, employee file, loan files, medical records, any other type of information that can be used to identify someone.

Your Specific Responsibilities under PIPEDA:

Comply with all areas of the law. Ensure that your business has established privacy policies. Be responsible for protection of all personal information collected or transferred to a third party. Before you collect any personal information, determine exactly what you will require and what will not be necessary. Inform the customer what the purpose is for its being collected.

- Obtain their consent before proceeding and record the consent being received.
- Limit the amount of information that is being collected. Do not deceive or mislead clients as to the purpose of the data being collected.
- Keep information only for as long as it will be required and for the purpose that it was collected. Have a procedure in place to ensure the information is destroyed after it is no longer required.
- Ensure the information you receive is correct and is updated as necessary.
- Protect all information gathered—regardless of in what form it is maintained—from theft or loss.
- Make sure your clients are aware of your policies for protection of their personal information. Create a clear and understandable policy.
- Ensure that clients have access to the information you have collected anytime they wish to see it (with some ex-

ceptions noted below *). Be prepared to explain how the information was used and be able to provide a list of any other organizations that the information was also provided to.

- Develop a complaint policy for clients and be able to inform them of what other avenues they can pursue. Investigate all complaints received.

*Organizations MUST NOT disclose client information collected back to the client if:

a) the disclosure would also reveal additional information collected about others;

b) if the information has already been provided to the government for law enforcement—in which case the client must not be told this has occurred and the Privacy Commissioner of Canada must be contacted.

Organizations may use their own preferences whether or not they provide a client with details of the information they have collected about them under specific circumstances:

- solicitor-client privilege (for instance where the business has consulted a solicitor regarding possible legal proceedings against the client)
- it contains confidential commercial information
- disclosure could harm the individual's life
- the information was collected without the person's consent, during a federal or provincial law investigation
- it was obtained from a formal dispute resolution process

Offences under PIPEDA:

- to destroy personal information that an individual has requested;
- to retaliate against an employee who has made a complaint to the Commissioner or who refuses to disregard the law;
- or to hinder a complaint investigation or an audit by the Commissioner or delegate.

The Office of the Privacy Commissioner of Canada oversees all of our privacy legislation including the PIPEDA. The Commissioner is an Officer of Parliament and reports to the House of Commons. In additional to publishing and supporting an awareness of privacy laws, the Commissioner's Office has the power to investigate complaints including calling witnesses and requesting evidence. If they are unable to resolve complaints, they have the additional power to take issues directly to the federal court.

PRIVACY LEGISLATION AUDITS

The Commissioner may, with reasonable grounds, audit the personal information management practices of an organization.

What can you do if a privacy breach should occur in your business?

- apologize
- try to correct the problem
- if it cannot be corrected offer some type of compensation
- assure the client that you will fix the process breakdown that caused the privacy breach (and do it)
- follow up to see if the issue was resolved to their satisfaction

One privacy breach can cause you to lose one client. A significant breach could devastate your client base and business reputation for years to come.

My Business Issues and Plans:

4.

Accountants, Bookkeepers, and Lawyers: How to Tell the Good from the Bad

What you don't want to happen

Marie, a very successful businessperson, was doing so well she was continually looking for new opportunities. She owned two separate successful companies and was a partner in another. Life was hectic, but she was enjoying herself immensely. Several members of her family were employed to keep things running smoothly but the bookkeeping was a nightmare that no one could keep up with. Marie had been dealing with a small local accounting business for several years and approached the owner for assistance. It was agreed that Mark, a bookkeeper in the office, would look after all of the daily business accounting. Mark would receive the business bank statements, complete a monthly income and expense statement, and manage the accounts payable. While he was preparing the accounts payable for mailing out he was given access to blank business cheques. He was also receiving the month end bank statements which held copies of paid cheques with the business owner's signature. Mark was in control of so much of the account information he was able to forge the business owner's signature on cheques payable to himself. For two to three years the bookkeeper appeared to complete his work to the satisfaction of the accounting firm and the business owner. That is until someone finally decided to take a closer look at the company bank statements. By the time all of his forged cheques were found Mark had stolen over $100,000 and had nothing to show for the money he had taken—it was gone.

How could something like this happen? Basically, there were two reasons:

There was no proper separation of duties. For accounting purposes, the responsibility of balancing the books, accounts payable, accounts receivable, and preparing the monthly balance sheet or income and expense statement should be completed by two or more persons. If that is not possible, the business owner should make a point to review all monthly financial records themselves. In this case, neither the accounting firm's owner nor the business owner herself verified any of the financial information prepared by the clerk or reviewed the bank statements.

No one except the business account owner(s) should have access to blank business cheques. If a blank cheque is required it should be obtained from a locked cabinet, which is under the control of a person other than the one who is paying the bills. What the cheque will be used for should be recorded immediately in the cheque ledger. The cheque should also be completed in full right away and not left lying on a desk.

What you do want to happen

Grant Foster's home decorating and painting business had grown exponentially over the past couple of years. He now had more clients and larger job opportunities than he could handle on his own. He was in the midst of hiring yet another new painter to assist with the overflow. One day he received a Revenue Canada letter in the mail, but it was July. He was puzzled as to what could they want at this time of year. His business income taxes had been filed on time several months ago. Surprise! It was a notice that his business tax returns were about to be audited. The letter indicated there were several "questionable" expense deductions that he'd been making over the past two years and they were requesting more detailed information. This was the last thing he needed right in the middle of the busiest summer he had ever encountered. Grant immediately picked up the phone and called his accountant.

Income tax audits can be stressful and complicated. If you've been working with a professional accountant they can handle the government's enquiry while you can get on with what you know best—your business. Often when you are audited it can mean a tax adjustment will be coming, along with a higher tax bill. An accountant has the knowledge to prepare business income tax returns year after year, despite the frequently changing government tax regulations. He or she will know how to deal with an audit situation and can help ensure any adjusted tax amount owing is justified under current tax laws.

When looking for an accountant, bookkeeping firm, or lawyer to work with your business, consider the following:

- Join your local Business Improvement Association or Chamber of Commerce. Along with the various business support services these organizations offer, you should be able to meet and get to know accounting or legal professionals through the group.
- Find out who is recommended by others in your line of business. Or ask any other individual whose judgment you trust who they use.
- Check each of the names you have been provided to see

if they are registered with their local professional associations (CGA/accounting societies, law societies, etc.)

- Also, check the Better Business Bureau to see if they are registered, and if so, whether there have ever been any complaints lodged against them.
- Meet with several before making your final choice.

BOOKKEEPING AND ACCOUNTING SERVICES

As mentioned earlier, sometimes a business is too large for the owner(s) to be able to complete all of the banking or bookkeeping on their own. If you still wish to keep your financial records in-house, ensuring separation of duties is really the only policy you should follow. For instance, no employee should have control of an entire process such as opening mail to receive invoice payments, recording of the invoice in the ledger, controlling the blank business cheques, and mailing them out. A goal would be to keep at least part of the business financial duties assigned to another independent employee. This helps to keep everyone involved honest. Ensure though that you still oversee the work they are doing. Accounting issues can definitely be caused by internal embezzlers, but often business funds are lost simply because of careless staff processing errors. Ultimately it is your livelihood that will be affected if they do not accurately complete their tasks. Never provide a bookkeeper or any employee with a signed blank cheque for them to complete themselves. Also, never let them know more about your business' financial procedures and practices than you do.

If you do have an outside accountant, independent bookkeeper, or a bookkeeping firm managing your financial documents, also plan to review what they have done. It should not be necessary to check every little detail of the accounting—if you feel you need to, you have not chosen the right firm to work for you. You can, however, periodically re-examine your monthly bank account statement and ensure the entries were recorded properly in the ledger. These types of validations can be done for different areas each month, for example, you can spot check accounts receivables or payables to ensure they match the accounting entries against your individual client accounts or computer sales records. You can determine how many balances and checks suit you and how often they will be completed. Just make sure you follow through. Even having a few key checks and balances in place may deter an internal thief. If there is opportunity for them to be caught stealing they may decide to try their luck with another business instead of yours. I should note that an outside bookkeeper should NEVER be provided with carte blanche access to your business account. If they need online access to monitor your account transactions make sure it's view only access where no transactions can be made.

If your business is becoming very large or you are thinking of going public you might like to have a look at the U.S. *Sarbanes-Oxley Act* (sometimes called SOX) enacted in 2002. This is accounting legislation for public entities that came out of the Enron, WorldCom, and other high profile accounting fiascos where millions of shareholders lost a significant amount of their investment funds. Canadian businesses that wish to trade their stocks in the U.S. are required to comply with these laws.

Let's take a brief look at these new accounting regulations that are now in place for U.S. publically traded companies:

The Act begins by founding an independent board with oversight of all accounting agencies.

Secondly, it details the rules under which an accounting firm can provide their services to any publicly traded company, such as describing conflict of interest rules and the need for auditors to be replaced with different ones after a designated number of years.

Under this law, senior executives are now fully responsible for the accuracy of the business financial statements. In addition, there have been limits set on the behaviour of all internal officers. Penalties for non-compliance were also established.

Additional enhanced accounting requirements were set covering balance sheet transactions and further disclosure requirements for internal stock dealings of executives.

The Act included a redefinition of the code of conduct for securities analysts.

The Securities Exchange Commission (SEC) was provided with additional powers to bar securities professionals from practicing their trade. Everyone who sells investments or provides investment advice is legally required to have training specific to their roles and to be licensed. In Canada, each province is responsible for determining its own training and registration requirements. For instance, most Canadian banks offer in-house mutual funds sales. All persons talking about *basic* mutual fund information with a client (including merely handing out a brochure) must have completed mutual fund training and hold a provincial licence specific to the bank they work for. They can then only discuss their own bank products. Investment advisers are allowed to sell all bank and other mutual funds company offerings plus different types of corporate or government bonds. They must have a higher level of training and a different licence for what they do. The licensing for a stock broker is more stringent still. In the U.S., the SEC has the power to completely bar a licensed investment sales person from practicing their trade. In other words, stock brokers can become permanently out of a job with absolutely no prospect of ever getting one in the same line of work again anywhere in the U.S. In Canada each province also has the ability to bar investment advisors both from buying or selling investments on behalf of a client and also from just providing advice, should they be found of malpractice.

With SOX, criminal penalties were set for fraud by alteration, manipulation, or destruction of financial records. A new requirement was put in place that the Chief Executive Officer must sign the business tax return. The Act criminalizes corporate fraud and tampering and provides sentencing and penalties for non-compliance. It also provides the SEC with the ability to freeze business payments.

The rules above don't apply to the majority of Canadian businesses, but if you're keen to learn more about business financial safeguards (and you don't mind reading a fairly large legal paper) you may like to research the subject. I have included some basic information on the U.S. Sarbanes-Oxley Act as your small business will most likely be dealing with at least one Canadian business that must comply with this Act. All of the larger Canadian banks sell their stocks in the U.S. and therefore must be in compliance with SOX requirements. While your business may not need to follow any of the SOX rules, you may find, for instance, that you will be required to answer additional questions concerning your business in order to qualify for financing. These are questions that your bank is required to know about you for SOX reporting purposes.

My understanding is that embezzlement of business account funds averages a full 18 months before it is detected, with an average loss of over $100,000. Why? Basically, because the employee, bookkeeper, or accountant is given the unfettered opportunity to manipulate the bank accounts to serve their own purposes.

I have provided some links in the Reference section to assist with your search for a bookkeeper or accountant.

Not all thefts are committed by career criminals. Sometimes a loyal long-term employee, perhaps dealing with a stressful personal issue, is tempted to steal by having unrestricted and unsupervised access to their employer's business income or assets. If they know that they may be easily detected by internal business controls that are in place, they may be less likely to steal from you.

TAX PREPARER FRAUD

Tax preparer fraud is committed by anyone who knowingly prepares and submits a false or padded tax return. Unquestionably, there are business owners who are routinely complicit in tax fraud. They know they are under reporting their income or over reporting their expenses. In some cases, the tax preparer also knows. I can't tell you how many times a small business owner approached me for a business or personal loan where I determined that they did not qualify as their net income was too low, only to be told, "Come on, you know I take in a lot of cash that I don't report. You can see how I make all my other loan payments and live well!" While it was actually a rare occurrence, it happened often enough during my 20 plus years working in small business financial management that these comments no longer shocked me.

I will not express my opinion on this practice here. I do, however, want law abiding, unsuspecting small business owners to understand that they can become involved in tax preparer fraud without any knowledge of it happening.

How might you know that your tax preparer has completed a false tax return?

- Their fee is based on the amount of tax refund you obtain
- Your refund is significantly higher than in previous years and you are told they found some business deductions that you may have been missing
- They will not sign the tax return with their own personal or business information (which is required by law) and ask you to sign the return yourself
- They ask you to sign a blank return before it is completed

Remember: it makes no difference who completes your tax return, the completion and filing of your personal or business tax return is your sole responsibility, including paying any associated fines for filing a false report.

LAWYERS

It is important that any lawyer that you hire to work for you has a background and experience in business law. This is an absolute must. Don't just select someone because they have been the family real estate lawyer for many years or because they are conveniently located. It would be especially helpful if they had an understanding of the type of industry you are working in. A solicitor, for instance, who has a large client base and knowledge of retail sales businesses may not have the expertise that you may need for your provincially monitored aquaculture farm. That's not to say they cannot assist you with your business legal issues and questions, but that they may not have any special insights to offer with respect to your specific line of work, and may not have the knowledge to caution you regarding potential dangers.

In choosing a solicitor to work with, you should sense that you will have a collaborative partnership (yes, that's what it should be) and that he or she will be good fit with your personality and business operating style. You should feel comfortable asking questions and discussing all of your legal concerns.

The best strategy would be to start your relationship with the solicitor right from the initial business planning stage. They will work with you to register the business structure type most beneficial for your personal circumstances and will ensure that you are aware of local licensing regulations, as well as dealing with any other legal requirements that may be in effect for your type of operation. There can also be discussions with respect to the legal ramifications of signing financing documents, contracts, or leasing agreements, and employment law to name a few.

Your province's law society can provide you with information on lawyers practicing in Canada. The law society websites allow you to search for a solicitor in your area. The websites usually cover frequently asked questions about legal services. They may also offer information on the practicing status of lawyers and any disciplinary history. I have supplied one lawyer search website link in the Reference section for each province.

Remember that, as with accountants, referrals from other well-respected business owners may also direct you to a knowledgeable and experienced business law practitioner.

My Business Issues and Plans:

5.

Hiring and Firing: Employee Theft and Embezzlement

What you don't want to happen

Twenty-three year old Angela was a salesperson for a high end women's clothing chain store. This was her fifth job in three years. The store manager, Keith, suspected that Angela had been stealing clothing on a regular basis. He had never caught her, but he had found her in a couple of compromising situations that suggested his thinking was accurate. He never confronted her or discussed his suspicion with the store owner. When dealing with Angela in the store, he was often rude and argumentative in front of other staff. One Monday, after several more pieces of clothing went missing, he called her into his office and angrily accused her of theft. He wouldn't let her explain herself, became very insulting, and called her a few unsavoury names. Then he fired her without notice or severance pay. Angela had never had a bad verbal or written performance report prior to that day; neither was she given an opportunity to respond to the theft allegations before being escorted out of the store in front of the other sales people. Angela hired an employment lawyer. The store could not prove that Angela had taken any items or that she had ever been an unsatisfactory employee. Other store employees testified that Keith had a terrible attitude toward her—one that they could not understand. They had heard his angry final meeting with her. Angela was awarded several weeks' termination pay plus her legal fees. In addition, the judge approved another month's pay because of the way she had been treated when she was fired. Besides having to pay these funds to Angela, the store had their own legal bill. All in all they had to pay out close to $10,000 to cover the costs.

It should be noted that despite the legal ruling, once Angela left the store, there were no further missing inventory issues.

What you do want to happen

Paul was the new manager of an automotive repair shop consisting of four bays, ten employees, and a fully stocked auto parts department. Within his first two weeks on the job, an employee spoke with him in private to say that he saw Steve, a mechanic, leave one night with four new tires in his truck. He thanked the employee for the information, but said nothing to Steve. Paul then completed a review of the parts department inventory management system and determined it was not working well. He made some significant internal changes to how they accounted for their inventory and sales. He also began to watch Steve more closely. One night he saw the mechanic leave work with several boxes of motor oil in the back of his truck and confronted him. Steve told him it was just an honest mistake and he brought the boxes back into the shop. The next morning Paul gave him a written warning letter which advised him not to leave with or store shop materials in his vehicle and to be sure to obtain a sales slip if he purchased any items. Later that month, while the inventory security changes were still being implemented, Paul saw Steve carry a small air compressor out of the back door of the stockroom and put it in his truck. He asked the parts department sales clerk if he had sold anything to Steve and when told "No," he confronted Steve and asked to see a bill of sale. When Steve could not produce one, Paul immediately fired him and told him to leave the shop. Just as Angela did, Steve also hired a lawyer to sue for severance pay. Paul came to court with detailed written records of his observations of Steve, written details of his conversations with him, and a copy of the warning letter. Steve's claim of unfair firing was denied by the courts.

Paul came to his new position with a strong knowledge of the legal requirements to hire and fire an employee. As a result, he had clearly documented all contact he had with Steve. That became the proof he required to fire Steve for just cause. More importantly, he had implemented the needed inventory security requirement that the shop lacked in order to make sure another "Steve" would not take advantage of the lax shop rules. Further, Paul made certain all staff knew that he would always ensure their anonymity if they were to report any theft or other suspicious activities they saw to him.

LABOUR LAWS

If you take the proper amount of time when you hire someone and you have internal office controls in place, you should have fewer staffing problems. There are a large variety of employment laws that you will have to familiarize yourself with that I will not delve into here. For a link to the Department of Justice Canada and a full description of the *Canada Labour Code* see the Reference section. I will note though, that with respect to the termination of employees for just cause, you should be aware of the following:

a) In the case of theft or any type of assault, immediate dismissal is permitted without notice or termination pay. You will need to ensure that there is reasonable proof that the incident occurred and you are not just relying on rumours or false accusations.

b) If the issue with the employee revolves around insubordination or the failure to follow directions, you are required to document several instances over time of when the problem occurred and provide the employee with more than one written warning letter. The letters should include the possibility of being terminated with cause if the situation does not change. The specific problem must also be detailed. The employee must have a reasonable amount of time to alter his or her behaviour. Only after these several written warnings are provided and there has been no resolution, can the person be fired for cause.

c) When it comes to the "performance" of the employee, in situations where despite their best efforts, the person is unable to perform their duties to your satisfaction, section b) above also applies. It doesn't matter why you want to fire someone, whether it's for serious insubordination or simply not meeting sales targets—the same process must be followed. You cannot fire an employee for just cause without notice or termination pay unless the employee had had several warnings and the opportunity to improve their performance or adjust their attitude.

In all situations, if you are unsure of the correct route to follow, be sure to engage an employment attorney to discuss the situation before taking any drastic action.

HIRING STAFF

In most cases, I would expect that prospective employees will provide you with a résumé. That may not always be the case, but if you do receive a résumé and are considering hiring the employee you should always verify the information that is being provided. Confirm that they have the degree that they say they have and definitely call all of the references provided. Have a list of specific and detailed questions to ask the references. If the position will be managing your warehouse inventory or working with cash, a Credit Bureau report or criminal check could also be appropriate. You may need a specific signed agreement from the prospective employee for some of these checks. If you don't have the time or ability to do this yourself, there are service providers available that can complete the work for you.

Take the extra steps to validate the employment history and personal background information you are given. This is a very good time to get to know the person you will be trusting with your business assets, clients, and reputation. If they can't tell the truth, the best time to find this out is before you hire them.

Office procedures and practices

Employees should have a clear outline of what their duties will be, which is something best done in writing. If you have specific ways you'd like the job to be done, this should be communicated. How are cash payments handled? Who is responsible for ordering supplies? Do they have a buying limit or need to get pre-approval? Does the office have a budget? Who will be accountable for it being maintained? When can vacations be taken? Who is allowed a key for the office? If you only have one employee or assistant these things would be fairly easy to figure out, but the more employees you have, the more complicated it can become. Make sure you spend some time covering all of the important issues. The risk of not doing this when there are no detailed work policies to be followed is that employees will make up the rules to suit themselves. You may one day find your business short money because of lax or non-existent office procedures. The employee may not have meant to make a mistake or cause a problem, but it will be your business that suffers the consequences.

Further to the managerial office process review, you could also make it a habit to periodically review your sales records. It would be a good idea to look out especially for a history of refunds to the same name or to several different names, but with the same address. Employees in need of some extra cash will file false merchandise return receipts or a cashier short in balancing their till may do the same to cover for a cash shortage. The same would apply in an office if you see sales invoices being mailed out to identical persons or addresses—especially those who record a PO box as the address.

With respect to cashiers managing cash sales, theft may also be the case for an employee who never seems to balance their till and is always short money, even if it is a minor amount like $20. Again, make sure you understand hiring and firing laws before you accuse anyone of theft. Smaller cash shortages are inevitable during busy sales periods or for new cashiers during their training periods. If significant shortages occur on a regular basis after a reasonable training period has elapsed, it can indicate that the employee has not been trained properly, they may not have the aptitude needed for the position, or they may be pocketing some of the till cash. I recognize that no one can complete their job perfectly every day and we all have times where outside life interferes with our work. Cash shortages are only an indicator of problems and should not be used as an indictment of theft.

For those persons operating an office by appointment (i.e. massage therapists, dentists, hairdressers) who rely on a daily record book to track sales, be on the lookout for reception staff not recording the client appointment and pocketing their payment instead. As well, previous appointments recorded can be deleted to cover for a new client payment taken today. i.e., the client record card will see a payment made last week with no appointment (a prepayment) and an appointment today with no payment (as last week's payment covered it).

A further note with respect to client files and records: when reviewing a file, make a note to check for their address changing several times over the past few months or years, especially where there is now an address care of someone else. This may be an indication that the client is not receiving any statement copies of their account or perhaps the records are being manipulated.

To illustrate this point, let's consider an office that offers massage therapy and physical rehabilitation services. It is the receptionist's job to greet new clients, describe the business services, book appointments, and record the client payments. It is a very busy office. The receptionist, Ms. Brown, has become aware that you have many regular clients who come in frequently and pay cash. Here are some examples of these types of record manipulations:

- Today, a client pays $80 cash and the receptionist pockets the money. She will then just go back and erase the record of the client's appointment.
- In a variation of the same theme, again a client arrives and pays her $80 in cash. In this case Ms. Brown now opens a completely separate *new* client file in a fictitious name and marks a payment of $80 against a *future* appointment that she has booked for the next week. If she is caught marking the payment in the new client file instead of the regular client's she can feign an innocent data entry mistake. The following week this mysterious new client cancels her appointment and requests a refund, which Ms. Brown provides in cash (to her own pocket of course). The real client appointment, not marked as paid from last week, is now erased as though it never happened.

- It would be just as simple to pocket the $80 cash, not record the payment to the account, and change the address on the client file. When the late payment delinquency notices begin being mailed out to the client they would never be received. It could take weeks (even months) for a business owner to catch up to the client to request payment for the past due account. Only then would it be discovered that the payments had gone missing and you would now have to decide whether you believe your receptionist or your client's story. In this case the cash payments taken would likely add up to a significantly higher amount than $80 as the scheme will have probably gone on for a few months before it was discovered.

Whether your business appointment and payment records are online or manual, what will stop an employee from doing this to you? It may or may not be easy for her to be detected. Are your client appointments and receipts balanced daily? Weekly? Monthly? And by who? You will need to determine what office policies and procedures best suit your business. Whatever they might be, ensure they are vigilantly supervised.

If you have employees who you have allowed an expense account, ensure that they have limits attached to the privilege. Purchases that exceed a specific value should need to be pre-approved by their supervisor (who should also have a limit, unless the supervisor is you). Review the expense charges monthly and expect to be given invoices or sales slips for all purchases. These sales slips should be originals and not photocopies. Lax monitoring of expense accounts can easily become very costly. For example, a highly valued business executive who amicably left a company after ten years of service recently contacted one of the office secretaries to request a reimbursement for an $800 business conference that he had been unable to attend. The secretary assured him she would look after it. Her first thought, though, was to review their account records to see if the conference organizer had already refunded the money to the company rather than to him. After some confusion and a couple of phone calls, what she found out was that the conference charge had never been paid in the first place! The ex-executive's reimbursement request caused the company management to review all of his expense statements for the previous year. Can you guess what they found? More than half of what had been paid to him as out of pocket expenses had been falsified. The company had been defrauded out of nearly $25,000 in one year alone. The company solicitor prepared an accounting of the past year's expense account discrepancies and requested an explanation or reimbursement for the one year shortfall. The ex-executive provided his own solicitor's response enclosing a cheque for $700 covering one "mistaken" invoice. The letter cited his ten years of exemplary service and an unchallenged history of charging executive costs as he saw fit. He noted he had never received any prior notice that he was filing improper expense reports. He advised he was prepared to publicly dispute the company's assumption of misappropriation of funds in court. Since the executive was no longer with the company, the remaining management was unwilling to have the matter brought into the public arena or spend the funds that would be required for further forensic accounting and legal fees. They declined to pursue or investigate the matter further

Some banks offer "purchasing" credit cards whose purpose is to manage employee business expenses. The cards can have merchant category blocking attached to them. In other words, you can block the employee's purchase of any items at specific types of stores such as electronic or jewellery retailers, if there is no reason for them to obtain items in such places. The credit card charge would actually be declined at the checkout if the vendor type is blocked. With a business expense card program, many cards with separate account numbers can be attached and given to different people. In addition to a separate monthly transaction statement for each card, there could also be a consolidated monthly statement for accounting purposes. This consolidated monthly statement will provide the complete data needed for analysis of company spending habits. It's an easy way to review operating costs and help determine whether there are any ways for the business to save money. It can also be an early indicator of office budget overruns.

You therefore have a couple options with regards to purchasing office supplies:

- Manage the ordering and payments yourself
- Entrust one employee with the task of managing purchases within a budget, overseen by you
- Provide several employees with the ability to purchase supplies, also under a budget overseen by you

In any of the above cases, use of a purchasing card would be advantageous, as the cards have built in limits, can be blocked to unauthorized vendors, and have a handy monthly accounting. A higher limit can be assigned to the one person responsible for bulk purchases. They are certainly not necessary, but if you have a larger office, the cards will empower your staff to get what they need, when they need it to get their jobs done.

CREDIT CARD SKIMMING

Credit card skimming is a major issue around the world and the situation is no different here in Canada. Skimming is where, during a legitimate sales transaction, the credit card is swiped a second time in a device that records all of the information contained on the black magnetic stripe on the back of the card. New cards can then be made containing the client's stolen information. The skimming device is generally a very small black box hidden under the sales counter. Some of the boxes are no bigger than a cigarette lighter, while others look like small hand-held calculators. Both have a slot where the card is run through just like a genuine credit card POS terminal. Credit card skimming is usually done by workers acting on behalf of a criminal organization. Sometimes new employees who apply for sales positions only stay for the few days or weeks they need to skim as many cards as they can. One day they will leave at the end of their shift and never show up for work again. They are actually already "employees" of organized crime factions. Skimming of cards is monitored by all financial institutions. Once a skimming situation is identified, the bank can usually tell at what business location the data thefts took place. In most cases, the business owner was unaware of what had happened. You may want to periodically check around each sales station to make sure you do not see any unusual mechanical devices there. Seventy to eighty percent of credit card frauds begin with some company's employee.

If your business uses bank ABMs or night deposit facilities to drop large deposits after hours it may be wise to ensure two staff members transport the money together. Firstly, personal safety from robbery attempts should be considered. Having to deal with two persons rather than just one may be a deterrent to a prospective thief who has been watching your business activities or the ABM unit you frequent. I am aware that there also have been occasions when night deposits that were made by an employee were then reported "missing" to the bank. If there are two employees handling the deposit the opportunity for it to disappear are reduced.

If you want your staff to assist you with your business account banking, do not give them your company bank card and PIN. I can't really understand why anyone would do such a thing, but it happens often enough for me to mention it. I've seen one day losses in the thousands. Your cardholder agreement stipulates that giving your employee your card and PIN is in contravention of bank policy and you will be held 100% responsible for anything they do. And I absolutely know that there are a few employees who would like to have some of your money. If you need someone from the office to transact business on your account, as I noted earlier, get them their own card with the access restricted to only what they need to do. You can do this with both client and credit cards.

Overtime is also another area where employees, if given the opportunity, may fudge the records a bit (or a lot). Managing and reviewing overtime hours is usually always worth the extra effort, not only to keep employees honest but also to keep the office budget under control. Punch cards were once used regularly to manage records of hours worked; however, this type of record keeping is mostly obsolete today. There are a couple of basic rules that will help keep overtime hours in check and time sheet records on the up and up.

- Ensure staff is aware that overtime work is not allowed unless it has been pre-approved. This would include workers coming in early or staying late without the same pre-approval. Time sheets can be completed and initialled daily by the supervisor (specifically to ensure they are aware of and have approved the extra hours). Be aware though that should someone actually stay and work extra hours, without the pre-approval you have requested they obtain, they must still be paid.

- If someone else is in charge of payroll, monitor the records to ensure no "new" employees who you have never heard of have been added. For companies with a larger number of employees, especially ones with many part-time workers, it has been found that internal theft is often completed by creating fictitious employees in order to take home a double paycheque.

An excellent idea would be to have a written fraud or theft policy in place and ensure all staff are aware of it. This could also include code of conduct guidelines describing how employees are to treat each other and clients. Make certain no one is able to say "I didn't know I wasn't allowed to do that." Sometimes what we believe are common sense rules are not so common to others (or so they say). You should provide a description of what constitutes fraud, dishonesty, and wrongful actions specific to your type of business. For example:

- theft of inventory, equipment, and cash/cheques. Theft can also include stealing confidential business or client information.
- falsification of records or misrepresenting facts to conceal responsibility for errors
- using confidential business information for personal gain
- suppressing or omitting important information crucial to the business operations
- hiding a conflict of interest that may harm the company
- accepting or seeking gifts from company vendors for special returned favours
- waste or misuse of company property
- the responsibility to report fraud, theft, or abusive behaviour
- dress codes

If you have a large number of staff you could consider an outside "whistle blower" call line for staff to anonymously identify other employees that they suspect of breaching any internal fraud policies.

You should ensure that any code of conduct guidelines that you establish for your business and employees applies to the suppliers or vendors that your company deals with. You cannot expect to enforce a one-sided policy with staff. In other words, if your rules state that client information privacy is paramount and one of your suppliers constantly drops off written invoices with customer names, address, etc., in an area where other clients have access, it is an issue that you will need to have corrected. If you don't do so, your employees will understand that your rules are flexible depending on who you are.

If you should find yourself in a position where you are absolutely sure that a staff member has compromised an important business policy, it may be an idea to discuss the situation with them before you consider firing them. Firstly, you will be providing the employee with the ability to correct any information that you have that might be inaccurate. Secondly, if they are later fired, an "exit" interview could provide you with the when, where, why, and how the policy breach occurred. The information gathered could be a basis for correcting any gaps in your fraud prevention guidelines or code of conduct policy. The interview should only be completed by someone who can remain unemotional and detached from the situation. There should not be an angry confrontation. My suggestion here would be that with smaller or less important issues, your best and most economical response would be to accept the loss and let the employee go.

I would suggest that you be cautious in attempting an exit interview if the situation is serious. If the theft or fraud is large, call your solicitor first (or the police). Let the police handle any interviews. If you don't do this you may jeopardize the ability of the police to file charges or your potential chance of restitution.

I can't advise you whether the police should always be called under these circumstances or at what point they should be called. Think about this—what if there was a physical altercation in your office where a client slugged you? That's assault. They can be charged and go to jail and I think the police should be called. But does that happen in every case? What if you weren't really hurt or you were embarrassed or you felt it was somehow partly your fault? I can say only that I have seen some complex fraud situations. Is it a relative? Would you call the police in this case or not? Do you feel threatened by the person? If you do, this is actually a VERY good reason to report the incident, no matter how minor the fraud amount is. Do you think there might be the potential of financial recovery if you call a lawyer? You may want their advice on the situation in any event. How will the fraud affect your business reputation if you report the situation to the police and the story becomes public? What would the effect be on your business if you don't report the fraud and it becomes public knowledge?

One of my thoughts on this type of situation is that an angry confrontational meeting with the fraudster may cause you more problems than you already have. It may also be detrimental to a police investigation. My personal recommendation is that frauds should be reported to the police.

In cases of employee fraud, a business owner should seriously consider involving the police in order for the employee to be properly charged with an offence. In many situations, small businesses just absorb the fraud or theft loss and fires the employee, perhaps because they feel embarrassed about what happened and want details of the situation kept quiet, or they are concerned about a public court trial and potential negative publicity for their company. Whatever the reasoning may be, if charges are never filed against the employee, what happens is that this person goes to the next office or business and gets hired again by someone else? Is this your problem? It could be. What if the next person you hire was just fired for fraud by another company that also did not wish to contact the police? If the person has supplied the name of their last employer, even if you call them for a reference, do you think they will tell you why the employee "left" if they didn't want to tell the police? These habitual con artists often move from business to business over several years stealing from everyone who hires them until someone finally reports an incident to the police. When someone is finally caught for a "small" theft of $5,000 a police investigation can often find systematic fraudulent activity over a much longer period. The thefts usually span several businesses and can amount to hundreds of thousands of dollars in total. Law enforcement officers are often mystified by the amount of unreported fraud that goes on considering business owners are continually looking for new ways to combat internal theft. Involving the police, when warranted, should always be one of the first fraud mitigation tools you consider. Doing so will send a very strong message to the rest of your staff that you will not tolerate theft of any sort.

As a last resort additional insurance against employee embezzlement and theft is also an available option.

COMPLAINTS ABOUT EMPLOYEES

If you receive a complaint about an employee it should always be investigated. Occasionally clients can be frustrating and unreasonable, but more often than not their grievances are legitimate. Don't let your personal beliefs about an employee interfere with a full review of the issue. The review should be done by you, the employee's supervisor, or an impartial staff member. It should also be thorough and well documented. There have been many instances where the investigation of a complaint has exposed a cover up of internal theft. For instance, a client who gets a bill in the mail for items they did not purchase may be told by an employee not to worry, that it was a simple addressing mistake. Or clients may complain of repeated billing errors. Any such issues should be fully investigated by going back over all invoices for a particular period to match the sales receipts to the bill the client received and also perhaps to others made the same day or week. See how many duplicates there are. Is it possible the sales person is taking merchandise or cash and preparing phoney invoices to cover their trail? You won't find any of this out if you don't complete an investigation and you just ask the employee about the issue. They will probably tell you that it was a simple error that they will correct. Best practice would be an internal policy to have all complaints lodged in writing so that none can be dismissed without an investigation.

Sales staff

If you employ sales persons who are paid on a commission basis or where their pay is in some way influenced by what or how much they sell, as a business owner you should pay attention to how they conduct their day-to-day job. These types of employees may be very eager to make a "sale" and are therefore vulnerable to con artists who wish to defraud them and, therefore, your company. Regularly discuss the employee sales efforts and the clients they are making contact with. Ask how, when, and why they spoke with anyone whose transactions appear out of the ordinary, i.e. large purchases, frequent purchases, out of town/international clients.

Most crooks like to get their hands on items that are easy to transport and sell, so smaller items and those with a good market (high priced health and beauty products, name brand clothing, and electronics) are often targeted, including merchandise that cannot be easily traced. They may attempt to purchase a large shipment with a bad cheque. You should also look closely at existing clients who have begun to refer many of their "friends" to you to purchase your products—there may be a scam afoot. It could be that the purchasers are receiving discounts from the salesperson that you are not aware of. Conversely, the salesperson could be the one receiving the kickbacks from selling products "under the table."

What other reasons might you have to be suspicious that an employee is up to no good?

- they never take a vacation
- they are always in early and work late without asking for additional pay
- they are never sick
- if another employee wants to help them when they are really busy, they don't want any assistance

The items above can indicate that an employee may be hiding something they don't want anyone to find out about. Mandatory vacations and cross training of staff between job positions reduce the opportunity to hide internal theft or fraud. In other words, if an employee goes on vacation, ensure their job duties are completed by someone else while they are away. Don't let the duties be pushed aside and all of the work pile up for when they return. Having someone else complete the job function may result in hidden wrongdoings coming to the forefront.

Other potential red flags that could indicate the possibility of employee theft or fraud:

- the employee recently appears to be living beyond their means—new clothing, vacations away, new car, new residence
- you become aware of excessive gambling or visits to casinos or race tracks
- you become aware of the employee suffering a significant personal loss from outside businesses or a spouse losing their job
- they have become overly emotional (teary or crying), or conversely they have become withdrawn or are often angry and argumentative. Further, they are reluctant to discuss the issue with you or their supervisor
- they have been a mediocre sales associate who suddenly becomes the company's sales "star"

Canadian Small Business Crime Stats

Percentage of small business crime types over a 12 month period

Average monthly cost to retailers $1,005

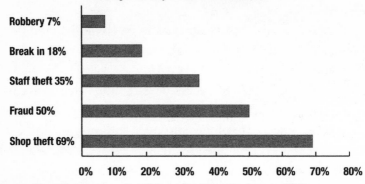

Source: News Release from Retail Council of Canada. January 2008.

Retail Council of Canada's January 2008 news release states that the average *monthly* loss to retailers is $1,005 of which $700 is attributed to customer theft and $200 to employee theft.

As you can see from the above statistics, a high percentage of business losses stem from internal theft. As a business owner this is an area where having controls in place will be worth your efforts.

The Retail Council of Canada has advised, in their most recent fraud report, that 87% of retail businesses were defrauded during the year. As for fraud statistics covering all types of small businesses, in total 66% of the businesses were defrauded in 2006, up from 52% the previous year. Shoplifting (clients and employees) accounted for over $1 billion of these losses.

The Association of Certified Fraud Examiners says that when an accounting fraud loss occurs, the average cost to a business can be upwards of $100,000 per perpetrator with there being very little chance of recovering any of it. Forty percent of small business owners who suffer an accounting fraud recover nothing—the average recovery is only 20%. Most of these losses are perpetrated by "trusted" employees.

Victim Organizations by Industry

Industry	# of Cases	% of Cases	Median Loss
Telecommunications	16	1.8%	$800,000
Agriculture, Forestry, Fishing, and Hunting	13	1.4%	$450,000
Manufacturing	65	7.2%	$441,000
Technology	28	3.1%	$405,000
Construction	42	4.6%	$330,000
Arts, Entertainment, and Recreation	16	1.8%	$270,000
Banking / Financial Services	132	14.6%	$250,000
Transportation and Warehousing	31	3.4%	$250,000
Oil and Gas	17	1.9%	$250,000
Insurance	51	5.6%	$216,000
Real Estate	29	3.2%	$184,000
Services — Professional	34	3.8%	$180,000
Retail	63	7.0%	$153,000
Healthcare	76	8.4%	$150,000
Wholesale Trade	17	1.9%	$150,000
Communications/ Publishing	14	1.5%	$150,000
Religious, Charitable, or Social Services	39	4.3%	$106,000
Services — Other	35	3.9%	$100,000
Government and Public Administration	106	11.7%	$93,000
Utilities	22	2.4%	$90,000
Education	59	6.5%	$58,000

Source: Association of Certified Fraud Examiners. "2008 Report to the Nation on Occupational Fraud & Abuse." Page 28
www.acfe.com/documents/2008-rttn.pdf

In most cases when employees committed theft or fraud against their employer:

- they had some work or personal pressure that caused them to contemplate the theft
- they were given the opportunity to do so
- they rationalized that they were only temporarily "borrowing" the money because they were desperate, that the employer "owed" them something, or that the employer would never miss what was taken

Usually the employee who perpetrated the theft was a trusted person. Employee fraud is typically accomplished by a first time offender—only 7% of business fraud is carried out by those who have prior fraud convictions.

Fraud and theft are critical small business management issues that require a variety of internal safeguards that need to be diligently monitored. You business should include all the protections that you believe are necessary for your type of industry and situation.

In review, all businesses would be wise to use background data confirmations for any person or other business that you hire or extensively rely on. As part of a general fraud prevention strategy you should also complete a review of your business office needs and establish suitable fraud protection procedures and practices that suit your needs. Any protocols that you establish should be reviewed periodically.

My Business Issues and Plans:

_____

_____

_____

_____

_____

_____

_____

_____

_____

_____

_____

_____

_____

_____

_____

_____

_____

_____

_____

_____

_____

_____

_____

_____

_____

_____

_____

_____

_____

_____

6.

Know Your Clients: Customer Fraud and Scams

What you don't want to happen

Dylan had been a devoted client of ABC Electronics for two years. As an avid teenage computer gamer he was often in the store exploring the latest PC games and gear. Dylan had purchased a few smaller low-cost items on his own, but normally his father came with him to make the more expensive purchases. These higher priced items were always paid for on his father's credit card. A new game had recently arrived at the store and Dylan had come in alone to look at it several times. One Saturday he came in with a $100 bill to purchase it. The cashier recognized Dylan and accepted the cash as payment. Three days later when the store manager went to make his weekly deposit at the bank it was discovered that one of the one hundred dollar bills he had was counterfeit. The bank would not accept the bill. As there were several $100s being deposited that day, the manager was unable to determine who had provided the bill to the cashier. The business was now out $100. As the store did not track or review sales paid in cash, it was impossible to say whether the $100 bill came from Dylan, as they suspected, or someone else.

What you do want to happen

A cashier, Jenna, who had been working at a large discount department store for only three months was one day faced with what she thought was an unusual transaction. A man was at her till wanting to purchase several new cellphones and some expensive electronic equipment on what looked to her like a very new credit card. Jenna remembered her training and followed the requirement to validate the card before processing the purchase. She asked the cardholder to sign the sales slip and then compared the signature to the one on the back of the card. The signatures did not look the same to her and neither did she see the three digit security code that should have been there. As she was hesitating to complete the sale, the man became visibly agitated and angrily asked her to hurry up. Jenna was not fazed by his aggressive behaviour and said she would have to refer the transaction and the card to her supervisor for validation. The nervous "client" had a few choice words for her and ran out of the store leaving the card and merchandise behind. The card was later confirmed to be a fake copy. By following the business' credit card validation procedures, Jenna was able to pick up on the sometimes subtle clues of a probable thief and saved her company just under $1,000.

CREDIT CARD ISSUES

If your business has merchant services and accepts credit cards, ensure that you and all staff follow proper procedures for verifying and authorizing charges. The RCMP warn that counterfeit credit cards are now the biggest area where business losses occur, more than genuine cards that have been lost or stolen. The card companies provide many tips for sales staff to ensure transactions are valid:

- all credit cards have security features such as holograms and logos that sales staff should be familiar with
- credit cards are always embossed with raised printing on the numbers
- there should be a three digit security code on the back signature panel
- credit card companies usually offer a 1-800 call line to validate suspect transactions before you process them

These are some of the warning signs that a credit card may be fake:

- the card is smooth and the print is not raised
- colours look warn or faded
- printing is not well aligned and logos are off kilter
- printing has spelling errors
- the card looks tampered with (signature on back looks like it may have been rubbed off and resigned or there is evidence that correction fluid was used)
- holograms do not change when tilted

More behavioural warning signs:

- the purchases are expensive (electronics items are high on the list)
- the person is in a hurry
- the person is overly chatty, jumpy, or is trying to distract you
- you have just opened for business or it's near closing time

Some of the fake cards being made are of exceptional quality and are very hard to detect. However, if you follow 100% of the requirements your merchant services provider has given you to process card transactions, you should not have any of these fraudulent transactions charged back to you. I guarantee you though, if you miss even one of the validation checks it will almost certainly be a loss you will be unable to recover.

With respect to clients returning items purchased on a credit card, you should always require that the original bill and the actual credit card used for the purchase be on hand before the refund takes place. The card needs to be swiped in the POS terminal for the refund to be credited to the charge card account. If a client should advise you that they don't have the card "right now" and ask for a cash refund instead you should decline their request. If you process a refund for cash and the original charge is later disputed, the credit card company is not obligated to accept the cash refund you provided as proof of repayment. They may debit your business account anyway and refund the charge to the client again. Asking for the original bill and the credit card (if applicable) will also dissuade people from returning tagged items that have been stolen for a cash payment.

Not many businesses other than financial institutions provide cash advances from credit cards but if you should offer such a service beware of bust outs or booster payment schemes, as described below.

"Man Drains Cash From His Credit Cards"

NEWS REPORT: A man was charged with money laundering and defrauding seven financial institutions in connection with bad cheques worth close to $1 million.

The scheme he used is called a "bust out" or "booster payment." The man legally obtained more than 10 credit cards over several years.

During a three-day period he made large payments to all of the cards with what he knew were bad cheques. Then he withdrew all of the available funds via cash advances before the cheques were returned for non-sufficient funds.

The man was arrested after one of the banks began an investigation of his unusual transactions and called the police.

The best tip off that this could be happening is that the amount of cash advances are usually large.

Debit card terminals are the same type used for credit card transactions. There is only one terminal where both types of transactions can be completed. They should not be left on counters accessible to clients. If the office clerk has stepped away from their desk and a client knows how to operate the machinery, it's fairly easy to "refund" a non-existent cash sale to their account in seconds.

TELEPHONE AND INTERNET SALES

There are special safeguards that are warranted for telephone and Internet sales. You will also need specific approval from your merchant provider to accept credit card payments via telephone and Internet, as they are at a higher risk of being fraudulent than a face-to-face transaction. These are generally the most disputed types of credit card charges and as a result the transaction will be debited back from your account if they are not properly validated. The extra authentication needed includes requesting the card expiry date. You will also be provided with other directions to follow specific to the credit card being used. Some card companies offer special online transaction verification programs where the client is required to provide a security code before the transaction can be approved. This is a separate service that your business will need to sign up for in order to have this additional protection.

Some warning signs of potentially fraudulent telephone or online sales fraud:

- large purchases from new clients
- orders shipped rush or to international addresses
- several purchases on different cards shipped to the same address
- someone else comes to pick up the item at the store rather than the actual card holder

Recently, a flower shop in my town received several emails purporting to be from a church in Ghana in West Africa. The pastor advised that they were soon to commemorate the church's anniversary and the congregation had collected donations for celebratory gift baskets and wreaths. The flower shop was familiar with Internet and telephone requests as they were part of a flower wire service that shipped internationally. It was, however, unusual for such international orders to be shipped back to the point of origin. The pastor provided several credit card numbers for the charges to be processed to. His information included the special card security numbers required for this type of sale. He advised that they needed to use several credit cards due to the card limits being low. Part of the deal was that the gift baskets and wreaths were to be transported through a specific company. The pastor provided the information of the person the shop owner was to contact to arrange the shipment. These extra shipping fees were also paid for through the credit cards. The store owner obtained approval for and received all of the funds from the card transactions. When the money was deposited into her business account she wired the shipping fees via Western Union to the owner of the shipping company. In the end, all of the credit card payments were determined to be fraudulent and the card company requested the return of 100% of the money paid to her, amounting to $44,000. The business was out $22,000 including the funds already wired for shipping and the costs of the extra product she ordered to fill the gift baskets. While she may yet be able to sell the additional $6,000 in products she ordered, she is not only out $16,000, but also the credit card company has cautioned her business and her bank account has been frozen. The matter is now in the hands of her lawyer. It is highly unlikely that she will recover any of the lost funds. In fact she will likely need to spend additional monies in legal fees just to sort out her remaining problems.

COUNTERFEIT BILLS

Fraudulent currency is prevalent enough these days that some stores will no longer accept $100 bills—some will not even accept $50 bills. If your business deals in cash sales it would help to ensure that all staff are trained in the detection of counterfeit bills. The Bank of Canada offers training such as "Check to Protect" kits, employee handbooks, and free training seminars in some cities.

You might be interested to know, however, that RCMP counterfeit currency statistics for 2007 indicate that counterfeit $20 bills are passed nine times more often than $50s and 13 times more often than $100s. This might surprise you since so many establishments will no longer accept $50 and $100 bills. It may be better to be well-informed and trained on spotting counterfeit bills than to regulate what types of bills you will and will not accept.

The newest Canadian bills—the Canadian Journey series—have the following security features:

- all bills have raised ink on the large number, the coat of arms, and the text "Bank of Canada/Banque du Canada"
- when tilted, the dashes (security threads) change from gold to green and tiny numbers matching the denomination of the bill appear. This is also true for the metallic stripe.
- there is a "ghost" image of the Queen's face that can also be seen when the bill is tilted
- in addition there is a see-through number corresponding with the bill's denomination that can be seen when tilted
- under ultraviolet light a section of the bill should read "Bank of Canada/Banque du Canada" and the bill's value should glow in yellow and red

Other notes have different security features such as micro printing where fine lines are actually made up of small numbers that match the bill denomination. An additional validation tip is to look for sharply defined lines in the printing—they should not be fuzzy. One series of bills has a square gold optical security patch in the upper left corner. The patch colour shifts from gold to green when tilted. Still other bills have small green dots. These dots are called planchettes and are located in random positions on both the front and the back of the bill. The dots glow blue under UV light. They can also be picked off the bill with a pin; they should not be permanently affixed to the paper.

In addition to providing counterfeit currency training for sales employees, the Bank of Canada continues to research new security features to include when revising and reprinting the currency. The Bank of Canada is committed to reducing the ability for Canadian currency to be easily reproduced. Furthermore, they work with law enforcement to eradicate counterfeiting organizations.

Bank note security features are easy to see and validate. Sales employees or cashiers should make a habit of checking the bills they are provided. The more your employees know and practice, the less likely your business will suffer a loss from accepting fraudulent bills.

Check out these web links for more details:

www.bankofcanada.ca/en/banknotes/index.html

www.bank-banque canada.ca/en/banknotes/education/ index_retailer.html

The Bank of Canada's website also contains fact sheets on topics such as identity fraud, payment card fraud, bank note counterfeiting, and cheque and money order fraud.

THE CASH SWAP

While we are on the topic of money, another type of cash scam involves two customers. One person tries to make a small purchase and pay for it with a large denomination bill. During the transaction, the person asks the cashier to make change for some other large bills and presents several more on the counter. He or she keep changing their mind as to how many of these extra bills they want changed and moves the bills on and off the counter. While the cashier is dealing with the original sale and the request to exchange more bills, a second customer causes a further distraction in front of the cashier and other customers in the store. The second individual may begin crowding the till area or talking loudly or angrily in order to confuse the cashier further. When the cashier provides the sale change the purchaser says she has taken some of his other bills that he placed on the counter and wants them back. These bills are not usually counterfeit, however, what the two hope will happen is that the cashier will become frazzled and make a mistake by handing back too much money. Anyone operating a cash register should ensure that money provided by a client is never placed into the till until after the transaction is completed. The bill should remain visible (but out of reach of customers) to ensure there is never a dispute as to how much cash was handed to the clerk.

ACCEPTING PERSONAL CHEQUES

Whether your business will accept personal cheques for payment is another decision a business owner will need to make. As noted in a previous chapter, fraudulent cheques can take up to 90 days to be returned—long after you made the sale. You can make an on the spot judgment call and take your chances depending on the client. Or establish a specific cheque cashing policy. Perhaps you may want clients wishing to pay by cheque to first fill in a client information form. If you chose this route, here is some of the basic information that you would require:

- Name, address, phone number, including how long they have lived there. (While we generally move several times in our lives, a steady residential address implies stability.)
- Occupation/employer's name, address, and phone number
- Bank and account details
- Date of birth
- Written authorization for a Credit Bureau check to be done

Please note that your business must be a member of a credit reporting agency in order to obtain a credit report. There is a cost to be a member of agencies like TransUnion Canada or Equifax. Their services are geared specifically to your business needs and so the charges are variable. In order to determine the costs, call or email an enquiry through their websites.

Any data that is provided should be verified or confirmed *before* a cheque is accepted for payment. Check phone numbers and addresses on *Canada411.com* (cellphones or unlisted numbers will not be recorded here). Don't rely on an answering machine message to verify a phone number. Unconfirmed fax numbers should not be relied upon either. Call the employer to verify the person does work there. Talk with someone who is in charge and can provide the employment validation you need. Bank account checks can be completed through your own business bank (for a fee). Read and understand what the credit report really says and means. Can you confirm the client lives and works where they say they do? Were there any negative remarks on the bank account report (i.e., previous NSF cheques)? Does the credit report indicate that their other debts have been paid up to date and on time? Based on all of the data you gather you can make your decision as to whether your client is approved to pay by cheque. If you do gather this type of information, remember PIPEDA rules for keeping client information protected and secure.

Do not let yourself or your staff be pressured by anyone to accept payment when you are not sure it's genuine. Refusing the transaction is valid even if the client is insistent and threatening to take his or her business elsewhere or claims to need the item urgently. Using many types of varying levels of pressure is a tactic to perpetrate a fraud.

If you are considering accepting a cheque for payment *never* call a phone number printed on the cheque to validate it. Bank branch phone numbers are almost never printed on cheques. Fraudsters print phoney numbers to call where you will get a live operator—someone they have arranged to answer the phone to verify every call about cheques they are asked about. Believe it or not, they always say it is OK! If you want to call a bank to verify funds in an account you need to call your own bank and ask them to find out for you. Banks will not normally release confidential information concerning client account balances to anyone other than another bank. If you still wish to call yourself, call only the bank phone number you find in the telephone book or on *Canada411.com*.

If a brand new client comes in and is already well aware of your cheque cashing policy this may be a clue to their future intentions. They may comply with your requirements for many small or insignificant purchases over a few weeks to "earn" a satisfactory cheque cashing history. Then they may attempt a large purchase with a bad cheque.

The alternative is to have a "no personal cheques allowed" policy for all clients, in which case you will need to have credit or debit card merchant services set up or accept cash only.

EQUIPMENT LEASING AND RENTALS

Lease and rental fraud losses can be much more than just the loss of income—your assets can also disappear. Today, what were once simple table top photocopiers can be very expensive high-tech pieces of equipment.

If you are in the equipment leasing or rental business, you will need to plan an approval process along the same lines as you would have to accept personal cheques. You need to be able to "hold" funds on a credit card pending the completion of the final bill for short term daily or weekly rentals of items such as constructions tools or snow blowers. This won't, of course, help you if the card is later found to be fraudulent or stolen, but for a legitimate client your payment can be guaranteed by the credit card company until the end of the rental period. What about items that are being rented on a monthly basis for an extended period of time? Cars, photocopiers, or construction equipment such as backhoes can be rented for several months or years at a time with regular payments being required. How will you determine whether the client can or will pay the monthly bill or if they will eventually disappear with your merchandise? You will need to develop guidelines to screen for the small number of high risk leasing situations you may encounter while not holding up the processing of typical applications.

A leasing business will normally have a high volume of applications. You will want to have a process where the majority go through a quick review prior to approval. Good clients do not want to wait days to know if they can lease the new car that they want. High risk and/or potentially fraudulent applications will have some key features that, when identified, should result in their being pulled from the usual approval process for closer examination. Some of these key features may be: out of province address or identification, PO box addresses, and excessive or unsatisfactory activity on the credit bureau report.

Just as for accepting personal cheques (noted previously), your rental or lease application should require a sufficient amount of background information for you to get to know the client and/or their business well. Of course, whatever data you collect needs to be validated. New start-up businesses are a particular risk: firstly they may not initially generate sufficient income to repay a term debt obligation; secondly, it is very easy to register a company, set up a new phone number, and to have business cards and stationery printed without ever actually opening for business. Stealing another business' name and forging additional background financial data can also be very easy to do. Of course, some existing businesses will inflate their financial data in order to present a solid profitable background to qualify for the lease. False financial statements may be difficult to detect, however, detailed application requirements that are verified, including credit checks, will go a long way to ensure you are dealing with a legitimate client with the ability to repay a long-term debt obligation.

For high volume leasing companies, there are computer software programs that are designed to weed out applications from the general group that should have a more in depth analysis or review. There are outside companies that can provide assistance with this type of screening if it is not feasible to have such a program in-house.

COMMUNICATING WITH CLIENTS THROUGH EMAIL

An additional office policy should be developed to determine how you will authenticate emails you receive from clients and suppliers. It's easy to send emails from various "addresses." Many people have several separate aliases or addresses with different email providers. If you receive a communication from catperson@email.com, how will you know that this is truly your client Mary Jones, though they tell you that is who they are? If the client is asking for general information that is available to everyone, this would not pose a problem, but what if the email is requesting personal records that you have on file about Mary Jones? The email could be someone else trying to obtain information about Mary. The same is true for your suppliers. What would you (or your staff) do with an email from george@paperproducts.com asking for your business banking information in order to receive their promised refund? You will need a process in place to confirm that email requests are valid. There is the option of using an outside secure messaging service where emails are passed through an authentication process where passwords are required. There are also various encryption programs available for sending and receiving emails. Any route you choose will be better than having none.

Secure messaging services involve a company providing business specific software to manage the security and protection of emails sent and received between particular parties i.e., confidential health information transferred between a doctor's office, hospital, and therapist. These messages require passwords both to send and to access.

There are also computer programs available for purchase that protect businesses from malicious threats that may be attached to incoming and outgoing emails or instant messages. The programs include anti-spam and antivirus software. They can also offer content filtering where specific words or file types (pictures for instance) are not allowed to be sent or received.

What about your suppliers? Are you at their mercy?

When it comes to suppliers, there is one main risk issue to consider. If you deal with a local store for photocopier paper and you buy products as you need them, you should not have any issues—especially if there are several such stores in your area. However, if you rely on a particular company for products that you need to run your business on a daily basis you should be sure to do a few things. Firstly, you need to investigate the supplier's credit worthiness exactly as you would any of your own clients that you allow to pay by cheque. This would include the background on the business or corporation, as well as the business owners themselves. There needs to be a reasonable level of comfort between you and anyone you deal with before you proceed with a significant business transaction. You must certainly do some in depth research before you commit to purchasing critical business supplies from anyone. You should obtain both a business credit report and bank report for them. Is the business in the local Yellow Pages? Contacting some of the company's existing clients to ask about their experiences with, and their opinion of, the supplier is also encouraged. Beware of any references that you contact who have instant raving accolades for the company. Are you confident that they can deliver the products you need, on time, and at the price they quoted you? If you need to sign a contract for a longer term supply, will they be able to live up to their future delivery promises? If the company's managers and owners are vague about their business history or capital and they will not provide any hard evidence of the health of their company operations or are overly optimistic and in a hurry to complete a deal—beware. If you do strike a deal with the company and almost immediately you find yourself on the receiving end of several calls from other businesses where *you* are now a reference for *them* you could be being used to set up scams on further unsuspecting companies.

Sham companies are often formed with the actual ownership being concealed; a young person, an older retired person, or someone who has never worked before is registered as the business owner in order to hide who the real operator is. These people may be paid a fee to be named on the company registration or may actually be unaware that they are registered as an owner.

It wouldn't hurt to also have a reasonable awareness of other companies that can step in if you have any supply issues.

Last Resort Backup Protection

Robbery and hold-up insurance, counterfeit bills insurance, or employee theft coverage is also an option to consider.

My Business Issues and Plans:

7.

Small Business Identity Theft: It's Not Just Personal Identity Theft Business Owners Need to Worry About

What you don't want to happen

Creative Advertising Wizards was the brainchild of 27-year-old Adam Washington. With his degree in advertising and sales, along with a superior understanding of the Internet, he was the perfect choice for businesses interested in expanding their client base through Internet retailing.

Within five years Adam had a client list that other advertising companies envied. He had initially opened and organized his business affairs well, but with a growing list of clients he spent more and more time dealing with his customers than paying attention to the office management. One of Adam's desires was to ensure his business operations were environmentally responsible. He always made certain that discarded paper was disposed of in the curb recycling bins, but first ensured that client privacy was protected by properly shredding documents containing confidential information. What he did not ensure was that the company's used business cards, discarded letters (some with his signature), invoices, and envelopes were also shredded before disposal. Neither had he put in place any specific office controls for the filing cabinets and business records. Often the cabinets were left unlocked and documents were piled haphazardly on the secretary's desk. Many times when he left hurriedly for a client meeting, he left his own office door open with papers strewn about.

When one day he received a collection letter from a credit card company, he panicked. The letter said Creative Advertising Wizards owed more than $30,000 in unpaid credit card charges. Adam called them immediately. He was sure it was just a billing error—he had never applied for a business credit card from them! Unfortunately, the issue was much more serious. The application for the card had precise business details recorded including a signature that looked identical to his own. The credit card company also had copies of correspondence written on the company letterhead with signatures that appeared to be his. All of the information they had on file about Adam Washington and Creative Advertising Wizards was completely factual, with one difference—the request to send all correspondence and bills to a PO box that did not belong to him.

Now what? Adam was going to have to hire a lawyer to help him prove that this was not his debt and that it was in fact a fraud. In the meantime, the bad debt would be seen on his credit record and probably have an effect on any new business credit applications. It could also have an effect on his company's income, if new clients (those who review business credit records before signing contracts) were reluctant to deal with him.

How did this happen? That question may never actually be answered. I can tell you though, that both Adam's habit of leaving confidential business documents lying about and not shredding his discarded company paperwork likely gave a thief the opportunity to gather sufficient facts about the company to perpetrate this type of fraud. In the end, the issue wasn't resolved for almost two years and cost Adam several thousand dollars in legal and other fees.

What you do want to happen

Frank and Mavis Butter began their custom woodwork business on a whim. Crescendo Custom Furnishings began in a small industrial warehouse on the edge of town. By the time 20 years had passed they were a highly respected member of their business community, employing 55, and shipping their specially designed products throughout the province.

Mavis worked steadfastly designing furniture pieces and supervising the various carpenters and assemblers. Frank was fully involved in the business financing, accounting, and office administration.

Early one Monday morning the company office manager, Pamela, arrived at work and found the back door to the office open and hanging off of one hinge. She did not enter the building, but called Frank Butter and the police. Once the officers arrived and checked the premises they told Frank that the office had been ransacked. They allowed Pamela and Frank in to determine whether anything of value had been stolen. There were smashed telephones and computer screens, plus several desk drawers broken open, but nothing of value seemed to have been taken. Frank was relieved to note that all of their confidential business and client information remained locked in the fire-proof cabinets. The thieves had tried, but had not been able to open the heavily protected cabinets.

Frank replaced the broken equipment and filed an insurance claim for the losses. He also added additional security features to the office entrance doors. There is actually nothing more to this story, since nothing further occurred. Sometimes we can't determine why break-ins such as these happen. We can't know exactly what the thieves were looking for. I once reviewed a surveillance tape of a night-time bank break and enter. The person moved back and forth around the inside of the premises (some of his movements were off camera and could not be seen). He left after ten minutes with only one piece of paper in his hands. I'm sure he was hoping for something more. An inspiring testament to the branch manager was that their important equipment and files were so well secured he could find nothing more to steal than one piece of paper. It is an enormous accomplishment—especially in a larger office—to ensure that every desk is cleared and all documents are locked securely at the end of every single day. I am curious though as to what was on the one paper he left with. I have to assume it did have something on it that he felt was of value or he wouldn't have left with it.

There have been many reports of personal identity theft in the news throughout Canada and these types of frauds continue.

Phonebusters was established in 1993 and is managed by the Ontario Provincial Police, the Royal Canadian Mounted Police (RCMP), and the Competition Bureau of Canada. The call centre collects information on telemarketing activities, advanced fee fraud letters (Nigerian 419 scams), and records identity theft complaints. They are the central agency in Canada that gathers evidence of these reported frauds, which they then provided to law enforcement. The agency also maintains fraud statistics.

Phonebusters Most Recent Personal Identity Theft Statistics for Canada:

Year	Victims	Losses
2002	8,204	$11,832,165.92
2003	14,591	$21,850,687.37
2004	11,938	$19,005,712.61
2005	12,409	$8,638,436.36
2006	14,332	$15,762,797.83
2007	10,327	$6,447,099.75
2008	11,091	$9,542,363.66

The chart provided indicates the numbers of persons that are victims of identity theft have remained fairly steady over the past seven years averaging 11,841 incidents per year. Annualized losses are $13,297,036.90 for the period. That averages $1,122.97 per person. You can see that fraud is a lucrative business for many. With knowledge of the various fraud schemes being used and employing fraud prevention tactics we can reduce these numbers.

What many people are unaware of is that the creditors who have been taken in by the scam are usually *not* going to take your word for it that you did not apply for the credit card or loan. While they have a responsibility to review the documents that they obtained to support the debt, it is often the victim who invests the bulk of the effort to prove they are not guilty of the crime. This can be an extremely frustrating, time consuming, and costly undertaking, so much so that there are now companies in business specifically to assist identity theft victims to resolve the problem and restore their credit record.

Public Safety Canada offers their "Report on Identity Theft" including information on combating this type of fraud. *www.publicsafety.gc.ca/prg/le/bs/report-en.asp*

Business identity theft can be somewhat more difficult to

carry out than individual identity theft, however, the incentive to accomplish such a scam is significant. The payoff from ripping off a business can be extremely lucrative compared to an individual fraud. While all types of companies can be the target of business identity theft, small-sized ones are more vulnerable because they often lack the resources and knowledge that the larger businesses have.

Business identity theft will unquestionably have a negative effect on your operations on several levels. There is the consequence of having a bad debt attached to your business credit record. Depending on the circumstances, it is also possible that there may be a debt collection legally registered against your business assets (until the legitimacy of the debt is disproven). Under these circumstances, engaging a lawyer to assist you would be advisable. Unfortunately, the time and effort required to investigate and resolve this type of fraud can be significant. Only you will be able to search for and provide the information that will be needed to refute the charge. Think of the lost hours taken away from your usual daily business activities. For these reasons, financially, business identity theft can be much costlier than personal identity theft. An additional negative factor: should your clients become aware of the situation and feel there is a possibility that the bad debts are really yours, they may stop dealing with you, which would result in a reduction in sales and income. The only positive side is that sorting through what happened and discovering how it occurred will provide you with the insight to prevent any future information security gaps.

TYPES OF SCAMS

There are many scams that can be perpetrated once fraudsters have information about your company, such as:

- Setting up a fake bank account and a credit card merchant account in your business name to facilitate processing transactions to stolen credit cards. In this case, one of the things they want to find out about your business is that you *do not* accept credit cards. This can make it easier to get a new merchant service, since you don't already have one.
- They may uncover sufficient information to apply for bank loans or credit cards.
- They may steal your good name and reputation to use your own or new clients in a fraudulent way i.e., selling non-existent (or inferior) products and services or asking for (phishing) personal information or credit card numbers for future frauds.
- They may decide to sell a "franchise" of your business (or your entire business for that matter) to an unsuspecting purchaser.
- They may use your name or letterhead to legitimize a fraud they are attempting to commit on another victim.

Along with your stolen business information, thieves can also use a spoofed website to make themselves look legitimate.

AVOIDING BUSINESS IDENTITY THEFT

What can you be doing now to ensure you do not fall victim to business identity theft? Chapter 6 covers many fraud prevention business practices; however, you may also like to consider the following additional tips:

1. You and all your employees should know how to confirm the identity of the person they are speaking with over the phone. If you are unfamiliar with them, check the validity of the caller by asking pertinent questions. Who do they work for? What are the business address, phone, and fax numbers? What is the contact name and number that you have on your company records? When was the last time they called and what was the transaction? Many fraudsters receive valuable information about their target company by calling and fabricating believable stories to convince staff to disclose information. Further, all staff should also understand what type of information should never be revealed:

   • *never* give out business owners or staff's full names, home phone numbers, home addresses, birth dates, or social insurance numbers under any circumstances

   • do not disclose when staff normally arrive in the morning or leave at night

   • do not disclose company vehicle identification (make, model, licence plate, insurer)

   • do not disclose company equipment make or model (photocopiers, computers, or other equipment)

   • never provide a copy of the business registration or articles of incorporation to anyone (except to your bank or for a loan application)

   • do not disclose security features of the office, warehouse, or company equipment

   • be careful to whom you provide the name of the bank or credit card company the business deals with (provide only what information is necessary and be sure the person receiving the information is entitled to it)

- do not disclose business tax or licence numbers, bank account numbers or employee ID numbers
- if you are unsure whether or not to release the information requested, ask that the caller put their request in writing
- don't be pressured by anyone saying you will miss a special "deal" or that the business credit "will be cut off" if you don't provide the information right away (if you are concerned this is true—hang up and call the real business using the telephone number you have on file)
- government agencies (income tax, PST or GST, etc.) and health insurance providers never call and ask for private personal or business information—if they need anything they send a letter
- if someone says they are "calling you back" to help with a problem—ensure this is in fact the case before discussing business issues with them

2. Ensure you secure not only private client information, but also your own business records. Shred or otherwise destroy any data you no longer require including paper and electronic documents or old address and phone records. Don't keep copies of résumés for persons that you do not hire. Erase unneeded computer files (completely and properly), destroy non-working hard drives, including old unwanted CDs and discs. Purge active computer hard drives of unused historical data by transferring the information to a backup CD that is kept under lock and key.

3. Periodically (weekly would be a good idea) search the Internet to see if anyone is using your business name, including using a name somewhat similar to yours.

Searching the net is especially important if you operate your own website. Someone may be using your good reputation or name to lure unsuspecting clients to a competing business website or for fraudulent purposes. This is known as "spoofing." I understand that there are website spoofing kits that can be bought for $100 and up. The kit is apparently easy to use if you have a little knowledge of how computers and the Internet work. With the kit, cyber criminals have the ability to copy your website right down to the exact images and pictures that you use, and download it to their own site. Some of these programs also have the ability to retrieve access codes and client credit card numbers that are being used on your site. Perhaps 80% of the spoofed sites merely have advertising related to your type of business where they make money when the ads are clicked. Other times the site is looking for you to "log in" so they can record your log in ID, which they will then use on the real site. This has been done with online banking sites. You should know that there is a software program that can be purchased that completes this Internet search for you by looking for any other sites that mirror yours. If you find such a site, you will probably need to work with various international authorities to get it shut down. Lately these types of criminal activities have been originated in Asia, Russia, and Eastern Europe. There are computer programs and Internet security companies that can be used to make it more difficult for your site to be spoofed. Discuss any protection issues and concerns you have with the computer or Internet professional who set up or manages your site. Please note, if you are operating your own website, ensure that your employees and clients know your exact URL. This will ensure correct access to the legitimate site. For instance, if your company name is Better Business Beginnings, when you access the site it should have the proper URL (i.e., *www.betterbusinessbeginnings.ca*). If the site address is spelled *www.betterbusinessbeginning.ca* it might be a spoofed site. If you are accessing a site through a "link" from one site to another (i.e., "see link for "Better Business Beginnings"), wave the mouse over the link to show the URL and make sure it is the correct one before you actually click on the link. Not reviewing the URL could cause you to enter a carbon copy "phishing" website where you or your clients may unknowingly provide personal information to fraudsters. An easy way to know you are always going into the correct website is to "bookmark" the page.

You should also note that fake emails that advise a particular computer program update is available, can also direct you to a spoofed website where malicious codes will be downloaded instead.

4. If your business account often carries large amounts of cash, consider having one account for general operating expenses holding less cash and a having a separate non-chequing business account where any excess cash is held. Businesses with seasonal sales are often in this position. Ensure that only you have access to the second account. This would help limit any losses should your business become a victim of fraud: if funds are stolen from your account it will only be from the main chequing account where a small amount of cash is held.

5. Check your business and personal credit ratings semi-annually to confirm that no loans or credit cards have been opened without your knowledge. The report should also

tell you what companies have requested a copy of your report recently. You have the right to obtain a copy of your personal credit record, free of charge, by mail or in person. This is a mandatory requirement of consumer reporting legislation. You should be able to receive a listing of all of the information contained on the report (i.e., any current or closed credit cards or loans and a list of all companies that have requested a copy of your report or credit score). You have a right to dispute and have corrected any inaccurate information you find recorded.

NOTE: All businesses accessing your credit records *must* have your signature allowing the release of information. Both TransUnion and Equifax currently offer open access to your credit report along with notification of any changes and various other credit support services for a monthly fee. You can check your personal credit report by contacting TransUnion or Equifax (contact information provided in Chapter 9).

SIGNS OF A FAKE WEBSITE

- Thieves always try to mask their true web address—look for a long string of odd numbers and symbols in the address.
- Look for typos or similar names in the URL or on the website itself i.e., *bellcanada.ca* instead of the real site *bell.ca* or *telusmobilty.com* as opposed to *telusmobility.com*
- The company logo looks too small, is stretched larger than normal, or the colour looks "off."
- Look for the secure site "padlock" picture on the screen before providing personal information. You should also see https:// in the web address (which indicates a secure website) before transacting any business online.

TELEPHONE SCAM ALERT SAMPLES (DIALOGUE AND WORDING)
False friendship or camaraderie

* "I understand you're concern. I'm a single mother too, just trying to make ends meet. I will make *sure* that you pay the best price and get the DVDs sent to you right away. We ladies have to stick together!"

* "You think this is a scam? Really? I agree, everyone should be concerned about fraud these days. I mean I was scammed myself last month. I ordered something over the Internet and never got it! I lost seventy-five dollars, so I don't blame you for being careful. Really though, I wouldn't be involved in anything like that. It's up to you, but I know there is no problem with this company—they have been great to work for. I think it's a fantastic product and I wouldn't want you to miss out on this excellent deal."

High pressure or urgency tactics

* "Your customer will cancel all his business with you if I can't get the information I need *right now*. Do you want that to happen? What will that do to your business reputation?"

* "Visa fraud investigations calling. This is an urgent issue—we believe a scam is in progress. Your credit card has a $1,698 charge being processed through it from a suspicious Internet business. I need you to quickly confirm that you are still in possession of your card. You do have it? Tell me what the card number and expiry date is so I can stop the transaction before it is finalized— quickly please, the time to stop the withdrawal from happening has almost expired."

* There is also a newer scam where a call is received pur-

porting to be from your businesses property insurance company, claiming you are in arrears for your policy payment. They demand immediate payment via credit card and threaten to cancel the policy if not paid that day. Also look out for related "insurance" scams where the caller advises your new car warranty has just expired and requests a renewal payment (along with your vehicle identification numbers).

An immediate decision is required

- "The offer is only good for this one call—no second chances."
- "Today is the last day we are offering this deal. Effective tomorrow the price will increase $50."
- "….a once in a lifetime offer that will not be repeated."
- "There are only two of the special packages left. They'll both be gone in the next five minutes."

Requesting information not required to be provided

- "I'm following up on the new accounting software your boss ordered. He forgot to provide the company business tax registration number for the purchase and warranty agreement. I've already spoken with him once today and don't want to bother him again. Do me a favour and help me out—I'm in a bind. Please find the number for me or I won't be able to send the package out to him today like I promised."
- I've also read recently of a fake police officer scam. The "officer" calls you from the police station to say he has just arrested a man who was caught with your credit card trying to "buy" merchandise from a local store.

"Do you still have your card? Yes? OK, then the one he has is a fake. What is your card number and expiry? I need to compare the two numbers in order to officially charge the person with fraud...."

Something is offered for free or has unusual pricing

- "Just call 1-*900*-777-7777 to get your free, no monthly service charge, office security package."
- "Congratulations! You have been approved for a free listing in our professional business publication."
- "Upgrade! Special business offer—five new office laptops for $999."

Cannot or won't provide a written request

"Sorry, this is a one time special telephone deal—we can't send you anything in writing."

Here is an example of how one of these conversations might go:

Them: "This is Revenue Canada calling. We are having a problem processing your last business tax payment. We need the social insurance number of the company owner, Joseph Smith."

You: "I'm sorry; our office policy is not to release personal information over the telephone. I have to ask you to please send your information request to the company in writing."

Them: "You want me to send you a letter? I don't have time to do that. If you want this problem corrected without the company incurring a substantial financial penalty you better give me the information today."

Cannot call them back or get their address

- "We have only outgoing telephone lines. You can't call me back."
- "We are not allowed to give out the phone numbers or address for the call centre—for security reasons."

Here is how one of these conversations might go:

Them: "Our mortgage refinance offer is for all home owners regardless of your income. A debt consolidation specialist will call you back to process your application."

You: "I'd like to call the specialist myself—can you give me his name, phone number, and address?"

Them: "I can't do that. He'll have to call you back."

You: "I see. What is the name of your business and the address of your website? I'd like to get further information myself before I decide."

Them: "Why do you want to do that? I can help you. We don't have a website—this deal is only available by phone."

Cannot confirm caller's identity

"Of course, we have spoken before, we talked just two weeks ago. I already confirmed to you our business address and fax number. I'm very busy and don't have time for this. Your boss will not be happy if this deal is cancelled because of you."

Unusual transactions or requirements

- "We don't accept cheques or credit cards, please send your payment via MoneyGram or Western Union."
- "OK, I understand that you don't want to pay for something you are not sure you will receive—instead I can authorize a 50% upfront payment and the rest when the package is received. You say that's still not acceptable? How about you send the $100 shipping and handling fee and then pay the balance when you receive the parcel?" Legitimate businesses won't bargain with you!

Fax and phone numbers

Calls appear to be coming from 000-000-0000 or 123-456-7890 or 888-888-8888. These numbers do not necessarily mean the call is from a scammer, however why would a legitimate company obscure the real number they are calling from?

In many cases the caller is in a hurry and wants the deal done NOW. They can also become angry, argumentative, and rude if you don't want to talk with them or you give them a hard time. The "nice" ones just hang up on you! Telephone scammers can also change their sales pitch depending on how much they know about you and what you have been saying to them. For instance, if they believe you are elderly they will be patient and pleasant. If they believe you are a middle-aged businessman they may become businesslike (i.e., strong authoritative voice). Their pitch will also change depending on the topic of the call. e.g., Happy and excited for a free trip or sombre and quiet for phoney health insurance. Those who agree to attend "free" seminars are prime targets for scammers.

A FEW IDEAS TO HELP BEAT TELEPHONE SCAMMERS

- You should be able to avoid most scam calls if your incoming and outgoing phone conversations are recorded and your answering message says so. It is Canadian law that any business recording their telephone calls must disclose this fact to the caller before any conversation takes place. If the caller remains on the line after listening to your verbal warning they have provided their unspoken consent.

- If you are concerned that a call may not be genuine and you don't record incoming or outgoing calls, if you tell the caller to "hold for a minute" because you need to begin recording the call— scammers will likely hang up.

- If you are unsure whether it is a legitimate call or not, always ask for the company name and return phone number. If they can't or won't provide this information you can be sure it isn't an important call. If you are provided any information, validate it against your own records, the local telephone book, or Canada 411 before you call back.

Even Dr. Phil has been scammed!

Several loyal viewers of the television program *Dr. Phil* called directory assistance, asked for the show's telephone line, and were given a 1-800 number. When they called they spoke with a person who claimed she was the director of the program. The callers wanted Dr. Phil's assistance with personal problems and were told that he would provide them with private counselling. They were told that a one-hour telephone therapy session would cost $375, which they were to forward via Western Union. Of course, after the monies were sent none of the sessions happened. Eventually the unhappy viewers obtained the real telephone number for the show and called to report the incidents.

Dr. Phil was outraged, of course. His wife Robin, wired with microphones, called the 1-800 number pretending to be a viewer and asked for a consultation with herself. She was told by the same fake program director that a 1½ hour consultation would be $475 or $1,250 to speak with both Robin and Dr. Phil. She was also told the funds needed to be sent via Western Union. Robin wired the $475 and then called back for her meeting with the phoney Robin. Excuses were made for several appointment times not being met. They then asked for more money so that she could have a conference call with Robin and Dr. Phil together. More money was sent. There were more delay tactics from the scam artists. After several calls and arguments between the two, Robin was eventually told that there would be no counselling and the funds would be sent back to her via Western Union to her credit card. The funds were never returned.

In the meantime, Dr. Phil had called in the services of a former FBI agent who was working as a private investigator to help track down the scammers. Based on the location of the Western Union office the money was sent to and name of the person the wires were to be sent to, the P.I. sets up surveillance. He also engaged some other individuals to call and wire funds. They found the 1-800 number was disconnected. The number was, however, traced back to a psychic shop in the same city as the Western Union outlet. The local police knew the store and the four women running it. Surveillance was set up and undercover people entered to determine what was going on inside. There were several women in the store, including the one whose voice could be heard on the 1-800 phone line. Another of the women had the same name that some of the wired funds were paid to.

In a reverse scam, the P.I. invited the store psychics to attend a bachelorette party to read palms. All four women arrived at a hotel suite. Dr. Phil was in a neighbouring room waiting for them with several TV cameras. He entered the party room and confronted them with their fraud. Of course they denied everything. In the end, Dr. Phil turned all of the information and taped calls obtained by the P.I. over to the local district attorney's office. He intends to ensure they are prosecuted.

See Dr. Phil's website for the whole story:
www.drphil.com/messageboard/topic/1990/5/

My Business Issues and Plans:

_____

_____

_____

_____

_____

_____

_____

_____

_____

_____

_____

_____

_____

_____

_____

_____

_____

_____

_____

_____

_____

_____

_____

_____

_____

_____

_____

_____

_____

_____

8.
Telephone, Internet, and Other Scams: How Businesses Unwittingly Participate in Illegal Activities

What you don't want to happen

The Internet is loaded with businesses selling their wares. For George, a very hard-working small business owner, this was where he saved himself a lot of time. One day he was looking for new business property insurance protection and found exactly what he wanted online with a well known company. After several email conversations with the sales agent, he agreed to purchase a new policy from them. The documents arrived in the mail with a bill for the year, which George paid in full. He also paid the policy renewal annually for the next two years. One day his store was heavily damaged by a fire but when he attempted to contact the insurer by email he could not get a response. The phone numbers he was given were not being answered either. When he looked more closely at the insurance papers he noticed that the name of the insurance company was only similar to the well-known company he thought he had purchased a policy from. He had not actually purchased from the known company at all—he had been defrauded. Though he notified the police, there was not much that could be done. More than just the annual cost of the policy, George found himself with $100,000 in damages to his store that he had to pay for out of his own pocket. For him that meant he had to increase his mortgage to get the funds, or close up the business.

What you do want to happen

Imagination Gardens Inc. was a very busy magazine publishing company. Many individuals came and went at all times of the day, so much so that the receptionist sometimes had a difficult time keeping track of everyone. Tuesday afternoon a courier stopped by with a COD package addressed to the magazine. Jennifer was used to having last minute COD orders come into the office, but today the messenger was unusually friendly and overly talkative. He told her the printer ink cartridges were ordered with a request they be sent on a rush basis. Jennifer had not been told that this particular package was coming and wanted to ask other staff members about it. The courier suddenly advised that he was on a tight delivery schedule and needed a cheque right away. Jennifer refused the delivery telling him he would have to come back another day. Later she found no one in the office had ordered any printer ink. The courier never did return with the package.

LOAN BROKERS

If your business requires financing, watch out for loan brokers who request an upfront fee. Not only could you possibly be providing a significant amount of personal and business information to a scam artist, but also you will likely never receive any funding. In most areas of Canada, requesting an upfront fee is illegal. There are many legitimate loan broker businesses operating in Canada; however, their fee is paid only after your financing is approved and advanced. If you decide you wish to secure any of your business (or personal) financing through a loan broker, find out how they are required to conduct business in your province.

For Ontario's Ministry of Government Services see the link below for further information.

www.gov.on.ca/MGS/en/ConsProt/STEL02_045977.html

ADVANCE FEE FRAUD

If you see an ad in the newspaper, on the Internet, or get an email looking for a local partner for an existing successful business that wants to expand into "your area," beware of fraud. The most current scam is to contact you via email and say they have received your name from a "friend" of yours who said you might be interested in a business proposal. If you should have your résumé sitting on an employment website, they may also say they obtained your name from that site. The email will describe their business, even providing you with phoney income statements or tax returns. It tells you that if you agree to become their "partner" in the business expansion they will then send you a cheque, say for $50,000, to deposit into your existing or a new business account. After you deposit the cheque you will be asked to send a wire, cable, or bank draft for $40,000 to a particular "supplier" in order to purchase start up inventory. The trouble is this is one of the many versions of advance fee fraud. As with all advance fee fraud schemes, the cheque they send you is a fake. Once deposited it will take days or weeks for it to be returned and debited back to the bank account, but the funds you withdrew for the wire or draft are long gone. Your new business partner has suddenly disappeared with the money you sent to them. You now owe the bank the $40,000 shortfall.

Even lawyers can fall victim to client fraud. On more than one occasion, fraudsters from outside Canada (or so they say) have contacted lawyers on the premise that they needed assistance in collecting a bad debt. They claim to have gotten the lawyer's name from another client who had dealt with them a few years ago. They provided the lawyer, via email or letter, with the name, address, and a background of the person or company that owes them money. The lawyers have advised that they would assist in collecting the funds for a specified fee. Low and behold, as soon as the solicitor sends their collection letter to the party, a return response arrives quickly with a cheque for payment in full! Of course, the fraudster exclaims his delight with the lawyer's good work and then asks that the solicitor to deposit the cheque into their own account, retain their collection fees, and wire the remaining funds out of the country. The cheque looked fine to the lawyer—he even called the phone number of the bank that was written on the cheque and was told the cheque was "good." In one case, the lawyer brought the cheque into his bank for processing. The employees in his branch knew very well what advance fee fraud was and called the real bank to confirm that the cheque was valid—it was not. The branch saved their client over $50,000. In a second case, a legal secretary became concerned when she saw who $250,000 was going to be wired to because she was already dealing with this same client and the same situation, but with another lawyer in the firm! In this case, the client was called to say there was a "problem" with the collection file. The lawyers never heard from them again. Another related scam is to have the solicitor manage "payments" against a private business loan or handle business loan start-up financing through a loan broker. Different story—same scam. Many professionals have insurance protection such as "errors and omissions" or "professional liability" that covers losses due to honest mistakes; however, fraud is not normally part of this coverage.

It is a business owner's responsibility to make sure they are dealing with reputable vendors and clients. None of us would be able to spot every scam in process, but the more you know about fraud the better equipped you will be to ruin their plans and not become their next victim. If you do lose money through a fraud you will likely have little recourse. It will be your business' bottom line that will suffer.

Beware of any communication or correspondence from strangers that:

a) says it's urgent, confidential, or top secret;
b) advises you not to discuss any part of the communication with anyone else;
c) asks for confidential personal or business information;
d) asks for money up front for a service to be provided later;
e) has significant spelling or grammatical mistakes; and
f) provides you with a cheque or draft that they want you to cash or deposit into your account.

OTHER MAIL, EMAIL, AND TELEPHONE SCAMS

You could also receive phoney invoices for any number of products or services that were never delivered to you. The invoices may not be for large amounts—perhaps $100 for photocopier supplies or $75 for advertising. In a very busy office these may slip under the radar and be paid without any investigation. You or your accounts payable clerk should ensure that all invoices match back to product packaging receipts or purchase records before paying any bills. Some of the businesses that send out these "invoices" claim that they are actually not invoices, but business solicitations or advertising or so the fine print may say. Others are 100% scams. Sometimes these rip-offs occur because office staff divulge information over the phone: "Hi! I'm calling from your photocopier service agency. Can you verify the type of equipment you have and the serial number, please? We are confirming this information to ensure your warranty remains valid. Thanks."

Some of these types of invoices are real companies using unacceptable and illegal marketing practices. These issues are dealt with by Competition Bureau as per:

"Misleading Representations and Deceptive Marketing Practices: Choice of Criminal or Civil Track" under the *Competition Act* (*www.competitionbureau.gc.ca/eic/site/cb-bc.nsf/eng/01223.html*).

Others are invoices from non-existent companies and are fully scams.

Note also that you may receive invoices from one of your usual suppliers where the bill has been boosted up from the original invoice amount. This could be an honest clerical error or perhaps an employee at that company looking for a few extra bucks.

419 SCAMS

Advance fee fraud is an age old trick where victims are asked to advance money up front to another person on the promise of obtaining future larger rewards. In the 1980s, a significant surge in advance fee frauds began originating from Nigeria during an economic downturn. The name 419 scam comes from the section of the Nigerian government criminal legislation that outlaws them.

The lottery win

Dear Mr. Fred Foster,

Congratulations, you have won the Irish online lottery draw held January 15th!

Your email address was attached to the winning number 57937813 matching seven of the numbers drawn. Total prizes awarded were € 1,076,000.00 (one million seventy six thousand Euros). Your prize was the 2nd to be awarded at € 436,000 (four hundred thirty six thousand Euros). Participants in the lottery

were randomly drawn from over 50,000 corporations, unions, clubs and organizations listed
on the World Wide Web.

For your security and safety we ask that
you keep this notice and all information regarding your lottery win completely confidential until the transfer of the funds has been
completed.

These funds will be available to you from
any of our lottery offices located throughout
Ireland. Our payment officer will begin the
process of releasing the monies as soon as you
contact him. Contacting our payment office is
necessary in order that we validate your win
and avoid any duplicate claim errors. Please
contact:

Payment Officer: Mr. Shamus O'Toole
payment-department@lotterycentre.ie
Fax # 011-353-1-2156-7645

On behalf of the management and staff of
the Irish Lottery Corporation, we congratulate
you on your win!

Yours truly;

Gerald Shaw, Lottery Co-ordinator

I can tell you what will happen if you contact Mr. O'Toole
via email or fax. There will be a request for you to "validate"
information they claim to have on file (your name, address,
date of birth, phone number, etc.). They may also ask for your

bank and account number should they need to wire the funds over to you. After they have confirmed that you answered all of their questions correctly they will break it to you that they require a small fee to complete the transaction. This upfront cost will be for perhaps an export tax, lottery tax, or a processing fee. They will need to receive these funds before they can release your winnings. If they don't receive the funds with their maximum ten day deadline, they will have to draw another name to win the prize. That would, of course, be extremely unfortunate for you. They will ask you to go to the bank as soon as possible to purchase an international money order or draft and mail it to them right away.

These people likely know nothing about you other than your email address (or fax number). Some of them may actually have a little background information about you gleaned from the Internet if you're a blogger or frequent social chat rooms. If you have ever been drawn up into such a scheme as this (especially if you actually sent someone the money they were asking for), whatever information you divulged will probably have been sold to one or more other online thieves.

Nigerian letter scam
Ibadan, Nigeria
Attention: Company President

Dear Sir,
This is an extremely URGENT, CONFIDENTIAL and TOP SECRET request.

I am an accountant with the Nigerian Petro Chemical Corporation and I have been asked by my colleagues to offer to you this most important business arrangement. We request your assistance to transfer $42,500,000.00 (forty two million five hundred thousand United States dollars) into your business accounts. These sums resulted from an over-invoiced contract four years ago from a foreign company. The action was intentional and since then the sums have been in a suspense account at the Nigeria Peoples Bank.

We are now ready for the funds to be sent overseas and this is where we need your assistance. As civil servants in Nigeria, we are forbidden to operate a foreign account. We will share the fund as follows: 75% for us, 20% for you and 5% for taxes and fees. There is no risk in the transaction for you.

If you agree to the proposal we will need the following:
• Your bankers name, telephone, account and fax numbers.
• Your private telephone and fax numbers – for confidentiality
• Your letter head paper stamped and signed

As the funds are required to be transferred out of the country within 30 days, we are requesting your urgent reply.

Best regards.

If you believe them and provide the information requested, again it will be sold or used for further scams. This particular type of letter usually goes to small business owners. You should know also, that if they have a businessman "hooked" (and they have hooked many) they will often ask him to travel to Nigeria to "close the deal." There have been a few true cases where the unwary (and greedy) have actually travelled there, were subjected to violence, and also got into trouble with the government with respect to their travel visas (or lack thereof). I've also heard that once the "victim" arrives they can also be coerced into providing cash payments.

A death in the family

Dear Mrs. Margaret Jones,

I regret to inform you that your great uncle Richard Westby has recently passed away at his residence in Rosemead, New Zealand. Mr. Westby's will clearly states that the whole of his assets are to be awarded solely to you - the charming young niece he met so many years ago. As the solicitor for his estate, I have been spending the last few months searching for you. I am sorry for the loss of your great uncle of course, but pleased to find you so that his estate can finally be settled.

Mr. Westby's estate is worth approximately $2,400,000 Canadian dollars. I would be pleased to forward this sum to you as soon as the minor issue of the estate fees is finalized. Please forward the sum of $3,750.00 by way of bank draft to my office address noted below. Once the funds are received the estate will be finalized I will forward the funds directly to you.

Again, I am very sorry for your loss and look forward to hearing from you shortly.

Yours truly,

Joseph H. Patterson
Managing Partner,
Messing, Messing and Thompson Barristers

If you send the funds you will never hear from the solicitor again or be able to locate him either.

There is a variation on the above where the letter is basically the same, but it does not ask for money upfront. Instead they say the estate funds need to be distributed to several people but they first need to forward the total funds to one bank account. From that account, various cheques will be distributed to others. They will ask for all of your personal and bank account information and they will pay you a percentage of the funds that will be wired into your account for your trouble. Of course the funds never arrive and your personal information will either be sold or used for illegal purposes.

A second type of inheritance scam involves your receiving a letter from an "estate locator" or "estate researcher." The letter will tell you that there are unclaimed bank funds from deceased persons being held by the government waiting for next of kin to claim it. They provide a name of someone who has the same last name as yours, but no other information. For a fee ($30-$50) they will provide you with a copy of the estate report along with instructions on how to go about claiming the monies. In this case there probably *are* unclaimed monies in the name of the person the letter indicated. Funds in bank accounts that have been dormant (unused) for over ten years are required to be sent to the Bank of Canada annually. The person sending the letter has mass mailed it to everyone he or she can find with the same last name in order to see how many will send the fee that was requested. The likelihood that the person is related to you is slim (unless you have a very unusual last name). If it is a relative, you could have gotten the information yourself for free.

Search for an unclaimed bank balance at: *www.bank-banque-canada.ca/en/ucb/index.html*

Deathbed plea

From: Mrs. Virginia Billings-Hastings

I am writing to request your most urgent assistance as I am presently confined to a hospital bed. I am told I have a rare and virulent cancer. My late husband Richard's untimely death last year has left me without any family to rely on at this unfortunate time. While we were married for 21 years, we never had any children and neither he nor I have any living relatives.

My dear Richard was a businessman in the oil and gas industry for many years in Venezuela. He profited from oil futures investments and deposited some $20,000,000.00 U.S. in the Banco Commercial here in Caracas. The money still sits in the bank awaiting my instructions. Unfortunately, I have been unable to distribute the monies in the account as I have been so ill. The doctors now say I may have only one to two months to live.

As a long time supporter of many charities and foundations I wish for these funds to be distributed to worthwhile children's organizations and hospitals around the world. I have precious little time to accomplish my dream before I die – please help me.

I urge you to contact me immediately to arrange for transfer of the monies to you. It is imperative that you do not discuss my situation with anyone. This is to be a highly confidential transaction as it may be thwarted if the authorities in Venezuela find out I will be withdrawing this cash from the country. Time is of the essence - contact me as soon as possible by private email VBH@network.com

My most kind regards.

As with all 419 scams or advance fee fraud, should you contact the writer they will again ask for many personal details and account information. There will also probably come a time when you will be asked to forward a sum of money to help with the transfer of the funds to you.

There is a similar letter circulating where the sender has become a new Christian and is also dying. They want to have their estate distributed prior to their death (as it saves on estate costs). They wish to celebrate the majesty of God and Jesus by sending funds to you in order for you to ensure it is distributed to various religious organizations around the world on their behalf.

There are hundreds (maybe even thousands) of these stories circulating the globe in just about every language.

Mystery shoppers

Dear Julie Jones;

We discovered your resume online and want to hire you to act on behalf of our company as a "mystery shopper".

Webster International Surveys, Inc is a top North American business evaluation firm. We work with many large commercial organizations such as Wal-Mart, Kmart, McDonald's and Tim Horton's. Our firm provides a review and analysis of their sales force and sales activities. As our mystery shopper, we ask that you visit the store noted below and process a wire transaction through the store's Currency Dispatch outlet. You will see enclosed in this letter is a cheque for $2,200.00. We ask that you deposit it into your account, keep $150 for your estimated 2 hours work and take the remaining $2,050.00 in cash to the Currency Dispatch outlet. You will ask them to wire $1,950 to "aunt Fran" at the address provided below. The remaining $100 will be the wire fee.

While you are there we ask that you fill out the following questionnaire to tell us how the service is.

- Did the clerk smile?
- Did they greet you warmly?
- Did they explain the service to you fully including disclosing the service charge?
- Did they perform their duties accurately?
- Did they thank you for using Currency Dispatch?
- Would you deal with Currency Dispatch

again? Would you deal with this specific
branch of Currency Dispatch again?

Once you have completed the wire, please
call us immediately with the wire confirmation
number. The completed survey can be mailed
to...

Yours truly,

David Roberts
President

Of course by now you should know that the original
$2,200.00 draft is fraudulent. Most of the people getting
taken with this scam are unwary young people (those with
their résumés online) who are looking for work. If they cash
the cheque, it won't be charged back to the account for a
week or two, when the account owner will hear that they now
owe their bank all of the money back. It would definitely be
an unpleasant situation to be in when you don't have a job.
Funds that are sent by wire can almost never be recalled even
if they were sent earlier in the same day. I am aware of some
being recalled, but the odds are slim. The thief got your call
about your sending the wire and sent "Aunt Fran" over to the
Currency Dispatch service near him or her to pick it up real
quick. I have five or six copies of these letters with variations
of the same theme. The paperwork is very appealing and
looks legitimate. In one case the package delivered was very
thorough—details about the survey company, the wire service
being shopped, and a full page of detailed survey questions.
The drafts also look very real. There was a flurry of these
happening during 2008 in my region outside of Toronto. I
was aware of at least a couple of dozen innocent attempts to

cash these cheques—most of which we were able to catch and stop before the cheque was deposited.

Summer vacation escapes
CottageRentals.Com

On magnificent Indian Arm Lake near Mt. Seymour Provincial Park and Granite Falls in British Columbia, we have four fully outfitted cottages available for rent. All four are three bedrooms with a complete kitchen, 1½ baths and living/dining room combination. You will absolutely love the huge wraparound porch overlooking the lake! See attached pictures of the cottages, rooms and the location. These are offered at a great price so book now as they fill up fast. Send your $1,000 deposit to ensure this fabulous cottage will be available for your specific vacation weeks next summer.

What's wrong with this ad? The cottages don't exist. Well I guess they do somewhere, since they have pictures, but the person who received your $1,000 doesn't own them and you won't be staying there next summer.

Maybe you saw the newspaper ad about the poor cute little puppy that has no home and needs medical attention? Want to donate money? Just send me a bank email money transfer to: *fibber@hotspot.ca*

There are real ads like this posted in the local paper!

These (hopefully) all seem ridiculously silly to you, but it never ceases to amaze me how many people continue to fall for them. The lottery one has been around for probably over 20 years. As the saying goes: "if it's too good to be true it probably is." Businesses, as well as individuals, can be the target of Nigerian (419) scam operators. I have read dozens of letters and emails with stories from the bizarre to the believable that are all scams. It doesn't matter what the story actually is, the key to every single one of them is that they want you to send them money upfront before they complete their end of the bargain. If it's not money they want, then it's your business name/personal name, address, phone/fax numbers, account number, and any other information they can get out of you in order to either raid you bank account (usually their first choice) or to use the information you provided to help legitimize the story they will tell the next person they try to scam.

Another more recent scam is a solicitation for small business owners to purchase a listing of their business name in a Government of Canada publication called *Canadian Companies Directory for Industry, Commerce and Trade*. The correspondence appears to be coming directly from the federal government under their corporate signature. Included in the letter is an invoice for $749.00 for the purpose of including a listing of your company name in the publication. They say it is information that the company has previously requested. This business directory is non-existent. The Government of Canada does not market business directories or solicit business. The most recent information available points towards this scam originating in Switzerland. As with the above, do not pay invoices received without firstly verifying that they are genuine. If you receive correspondence from the federal government check the name and address on the Government of Canada website: *www.gc.ca*. Anyone receiving this type of invoice can send their complaint to the Competition Bureau, who will forward it to the Swiss authorities.

www.competitionbureau.gc.ca/eic/site/cb-bc.nsf/eng/00157.html

Telephone: 819-997-4282
Toll-free: 1-800-348-5358 (Canada)
Toll-free TTY: 1-800-642-3844 (for hearing-impaired only)
Email: *compbureau@cb-bc.gc.ca*
Fax: 819-997-0324
Mailing Address:
50 Victoria Street
Gatineau, Quebec, K1A 0C9

In the last few years there has been a new health and safety related scam. A person contacts you to say they are going to help you out by selling you first aid kits that are now mandatory for businesses to have. They tell you that there was a Government of Canada Heath Agency law that was recently passed and it is now mandatory that all businesses have these kits. If you agree, you will receive the highly overpriced kits, however, you should know that there is no such new law.

You might also want to warn your staff not to make or return any telephone calls to 1-900, 1-976, or 809 numbers. I have heard of office phone lines being left messages that beg a return call such as: "This is Francine. I need to tell you something. It's very important that you call me right away." The recipient may not know a Francine, but believes that the message may nevertheless be something important. If you phone these numbers you are often held on the line for an abnormally long message before you get to a live operator. Once you get to the operator they will usually want to sell you something. These telephone numbers will have a minimum charge of around $35 that will be added to your phone bill if you call them back. Remember, 1-900 numbers have a per-minute rate. While there are legitimate businesses using 1-900 phone lines, the point of this scam is to collect the phone charges from you. These phone numbers are not the same as the 1-800, 1-888, and 877 lines which are toll-free.

A different telephone scam is where an automated message is left that asks the recipient to press a code such as * # 9 to reply to the call. If you do this, you may be allowing a fraudster access to your phone line. They will then begin using the line to complete numerous long distance calls (mostly overseas ones). The calls will be charged to your phone bill and you will likely not find out anything about what is happening until the next month's bill arrives.

In January 2009, the *Hamilton Spectator* published an account of long distance theft. Hackers broke into a local law firm's voicemail messaging system and the business ended up with a telephone bill close to $200,000. Bell Canada believes that the hackers used an automated dialler looking specifically for a voicemail answer. The dialler then inputs password after password hoping to come up with the one assigned to the phone. If they can guess it correctly they will gain access to the system controls and will then change the phone options to allow outbound long distance calls. When you get the bill it looks like all of the calls originated directly from your own internal phone system. This also happened a few years ago at a branch of the bank that I work for. They received bills over a two month period with thousands of dollars charged for calls to Asia. You should be aware that the telephone company does not refund you the costs of these calls—though they will make some concessions. Codes like 1-2-3-4 should not be used if you want to ensure your system will not be compromised. Perhaps they also ought to be changed regularly, just as they are for computers.

SMISHING

With more and more cellphones and other wireless hand-held devices being used, scammers have begun moving into text messaging territory. Common text messages take on the same form as fraudulent email messages, for instance, asking you to call a phone number to restore a locked bank account. As with the original email scam, if you respond you are asked to provide confidential personal banking information. No bank or financial institution will ever ask you to reveal such information over the phone or the Internet. A variation on the texting con would be to send you a communication with a URL that you are asked to visit. Some of these URLs will automatically download a Trojan horse to your computer. (These will be discussed in the next section.) Unless you know the sender, it is safer to just delete the message.

MALICIOUS SOFTWARE (MALWARE)

There is always a risk to the security of your company data if your employees are using their work computers to visit non-business websites—especially if they are downloading anything off an unknown site. Sometimes malware will request installation agreements or may employ trickery to gain privileges on the computer. Employees loading computer files that they brought from home can also have viruses or worms that will transfer an infection to a business computer. Any malicious software could cause slowing of system resources, crashes, lost data, and irreparable harm to your hardware. Further, your business reputation could be damaged on the Internet if a disclosure of private records or client files should occur.

Adware is a virus that often accompanies normal installations such as web browsers, or client files with plug-ins. Adware displays advertisements on your desktop, changes your home page, and inputs new favourites or links on menus. Somewhat an annoyance, these will hurt computer productivity by limiting resources and diverting attention away from work. Advertisements will be cycled in a click by click basis. Look in your add/remove programs to find the advertisement listed or download and install adware monitoring software to solve this problem.

Spyware is an information security threat that will monitor your activity while connected to the Internet. Once installed, this software will attempt to access your Internet usage, including website addresses and email. This is not limited to employee surveillance. It could recover deleted information, or monitor passwords. If a laptop has a camera, this may be used covertly to take pictures of what is in plain sight. Anti-spyware software is needed to regularly scan your hard discs for any threats.

Malware is an illegal attempt by software to distribute planned vandalism or denial-of-service attacks. These may be called "botnets" when software will run covertly in a background process, only to launch an attack on other businesses on the Internet. System resources could be compromised. The malware could be doing things without your knowledge, such as sending spam, which could be subject to criminal proceedings, depending on your locale. Allowing others to use your resources in this manner is generally considered illegal. Adware/Spyware/Malware are not included with your operating system—they are infectious and will continue to spread undeterred.

Phishing is new age fishing. In this case, scammers use emails, telephone calls, letters, and fake websites as bait. Those using phishing pretend to be a person or business known to you, such as your bank. They are usually looking for personal information that can be used to raid your accounts or credit cards. They are also found on social networking sites asking for personal information for identity theft purposes. Around the world billions of dollars are stolen every year through phishing.

Denial of Service (DoS) attacks are generally aimed at high profile business websites. Thousands of contact requests are sent simultaneously and continuously in order to significantly slow down or crash the site, leaving many unhappy clients.

A *trojan horse* is software designed to give administrative control of a computer operating system or resources for use in a variety of illegal activities on the Internet. This is done by someone inside a system (often by mistake), or through phishing (attempting to use social engineering or trickery to have passwords stolen) on your network. These hacking attempts allow a third party to limitlessly administer software to suit their purposes from running background programs or distributing widespread denial of service attacks (DoS). These could routinely install fresh adware, spyware, malware, and viruses until the individual computer is removed from the network entirely and serviced by a computer technician.

If you encounter a *computer virus or worm*, first contact will be through email servers, web servers, forums, or from infected computers connected to the Internet. Computer viruses and worms are weaknesses in your operating system created by software engineering to maliciously cause harm to networks and computer hardware or infrastructure. A worm is not installed by an employee, or through trickery or any other social advantage. These are only going to affect specific operating systems and may first be found on your local hard discs (temporary folders may keep copies of almost everything visited or installed as duplicates of infections). If a worm is circulating the Web (check technology news feeds) and if no patch of software has become available you should disconnect all unneeded computers from the Internet and contact your Internet service provider for updates until the threat is thwarted. This type of attack is preventable only through regularly updating your operating system. Anti-virus software should scan for old threats still circulating through unprotected computers.

Your employees must have anti-virus software installed on every computer. While several are available at no cost, they may not be applicable to business uses. These software providers should be evaluated based on cost and the number of updates per day. Technical support of software may be part of a package. Usually, a licence is given per computer, with costs decreasing as more computers have the software installed. A network administrator would ideally have both WAN and LAN hardware such as firewalls or switches. A software firewall solution should limit employee activity to only specific websites and prohibit program usage such as instant messaging or games.

Most importantly, the user will need basic training that identification on the Internet must remain anonymous, as attacks may be launched just from knowing a business IP address. Please have employees search for technical support through well-known search engines before asking a question anywhere on the Internet. If employees are having computer function issues, they should search the Internet for *existing* solutions to *known* problems. Technical support experts usually expect that this be done before contacting them. If they are unable to find an answer to their question they should not engage unfamiliar "support" information offers. Some of these support offers come from websites that will offer you a virus download along with their supposed advice. If you don't want your employees searching the Internet for computer support you should have the expertise in house.

CUSTOMER SERVICE

If you have a company web site, a "contact us" link on your site is vital. Why do you need a web site contact link? Customers will want to be sure your company is legitimate before doing business. You will need to provide access information to a person with whom the client can speak with other than online. Support ticket software is essential to keep apprised of current issues with your clients.

Support ticket software is a tracking system that will tell a business owner:

- which client called/emailed
- what the problem was
- which customer service representative answered the initial and any subsequent calls
- what was done (or not done) in response to the client contact and how the issue was resolved

There is a "ticket" number assigned to each client contact that records all of the pertinent information. If the client calls back later and a new client service rep. takes the call, the client does not have to repeat their problem again—all of the relevant information can be seen online via the ticket number assigned. Besides being an excellent tool that can increase client satisfaction, support ticket software will also provide the businesses with a record of typical and/or systemic issues which will help you determine if any modifications need to be considered in the products or services that your business supplies.

Most clients would enjoy talking to a real person before

being told to visit a website, but some may be willing to do the work themselves provided a FAQ (frequently asked questions) is available along with a search of forums for problems already solved.

Internet security research completed in 2007 noted that hackers and computer-based scam artists have begun using businesslike methods to gain access to home and company PCs. Various types of phishing programs are for sale in the "underground" to help fraudsters accomplish their attacks more quickly and easily. Some of these programs can effortlessly set up phoney websites that closely match legitimate ones. Over the past few years more and more of these scams have been discovered, targeting victims through online sites that mimic well-known financial, business, and employment websites. Sometimes just entering their phoney site is enough for a malicious worm to be downloaded to your computer.

These days the information stolen from you such as your name, bank, and account number can be bought or sold underground for as little as $10. Credit card numbers can be bought in bulk for 50 cents each. Your stolen identification can go for not much more than $1.

ARE YOU AWARE AND PREPARED?

A recent survey by Visa Canada found that only 25% of store managers believe their businesses are somewhat vulnerable to credit card fraud, and only 31% train their staff in fraud-reduction procedures when they experience a problem.

Marketing fraud and economic crimes such as embezzlement have put billions of dollars of cash in the pockets of crooks. It is estimated that over half of all businesses have suffered a loss directly related to these types of crimes. Some 60% of the thefts are committed by your own employees, with organized crime rings accounting for the rest. Being vigilant and keeping up to date on fraud schemes both internal and external will be of tremendous value to the success of any businesses.

Always protect your business and personal information!

My Business Issues and Plans:

9.
Who's Working to Help Small Business Fight Fraud?: Where You Can Get More Information

Small business is a significant contributor to the Canadian economy. Industry Canada advises that in 2006, businesses with less than 50 employees accounted for 23% of Canada's total GDP (gross domestic product). In 2007 there were 2.6 million self-employed persons. Total net employment growth in the private sector has ranged from 9% to 52% per year between 1996 and 2007.

As Canadian small businesses are an important segment of our country and society, there are numerous government or private enterprises that offer business owners support services. Several are government funded and free. Here is a list of those that proffer a great wealth of information. At a minimum, I would advise you to at least investigate what they have to offer. Just use your common sense as to which services will benefit you and which may not.

For more detailed information on the economic contributions of Canadian small business, consult the small business section of the Industry Canada website (*www.ic.gc.ca*).

THE COMPETITION BUREAU OF CANADA

The Competition Bureau is a Government of Canada organization that was formed to support small business and consumers by managing Canada's consumer competition and marketing laws. They provide small business with information on their responsibility with respect to the Canadian competition and consumer protection laws. The bureau has assisted with charges being brought against a Quebec business directory telemarketer who was estimated to have bilked 10,000 businesses, schools, and non-profit organizations out of $4 million. They also were involved in criminal charges faced by two Toronto companies for photocopier toner supply invoices sent to businesses and also government agencies in Canada and the United States for products that were not wanted and not ordered. A further case resulted in jail time for four with respect to phoney invoices that looked like they were from Bell Canada and the Yellow Pages, but were actually solicitations for listings in Internet directories.

Some of the anti-competition matters the Bureau investigates include price fixing, false or misleading representations, and deceptive marketing. Besides their operations within Canada, they also work with several like-minded international organizations. The Competition Bureau also investigates tied selling.

Tied selling relates to a Canadian law that states a business cannot sell a product under the condition that another must also be purchased or that the original purchase will be rejected if the second item is not also purchased. For instance, if a lender advises you that you are approved for a car loan but you will not be able to get the loan unless you also agree to pay for life insurance, this is tied selling and it is illegal.

Fraud is such a significant issue that they also helped create the Fraud Prevention Forum (FPF). Group members include business owners, government organizations, consumers, and police agencies all of whom are dedicated to fraud prevention.

Corporate Compliance Programs

www.competitionbureau.gc.ca/epic/site/cb-bc.nsf/en/02732e.html

Facts on Fraud Targeting Businesses and Not-For-Profit Organizations

www.competitionbureau.gc.ca/epic/site/cb-bc.nsf/en/02631e.html

Fraud Awareness Fact Sheet for Small and Medium-Sized Enterprises

www.competitionbureau.gc.ca/epic/site/cb-bc.nsf/en/02051e.html

The Competition Bureau's page entitled "Fraud Awareness for Commercial Targets" is also worth checking out. This particular site would be a great one to add as a favourite on your computer. While you may be spending a significant amount of time and effort to protect your company from fraud, it is imperative that your employees also understand what scams are and how to detect them. Each of the sections explains perfectly the various types of business fraud. Reviewing the sections with employees would be a great training exercise. Encourage your employees to visit the site to read:

- Scam techniques
- What makes your organization vulnerable
- How to spot phoney emails
- Victim stories
- Examples of phoney telemarketing calls
- Phoney invoices
- Telemarketing scam scripts

- Building an anti-fraud plan
- Report a possible scam

The real life samples included are excellent tools to ensure everyone understands. The information on the site is relevant to small business and is updated as needed.

Also be sure to check out the Competiton Bureau's Fraud Prevention Forum, also on their website.

INDUSTRY CANADA

Industry Canada works with business with respect to innovation and developing business capability. Their mandate is threefold: "a fair, efficient and competitive marketplace; an innovative economy; competitive industry and sustainable communities."

Their assistance for businesses includes detailed information on:

- Business tools and resources
- Company directories
- Economic, market research, and statistics
- Financing
- Innovation, research, science, and technology
- Intellectual property
- Radio, spectrum, and telecommunications
- Regional and rural development
- Sustainability and environment
- Trade and investment

www.ic.gc.ca/epic/site/ic1.nsf/en/h_00006e.html

The sections on scams and fraud on the website are also great for staff training. You can find:

- Spam IQ Test
- Fraud Quiz
- Fraud Files
- Protecting Yourself Against Debit Card Fraud
  www.ic.gc.ca/epic/site/oca-bc.nsf/en/h_ca02228e.html

CANADA'S OFFICE OF CONSUMER AFFAIRS (OCA)

A division of Industry Canada detailed with protecting consumers within the marketplace. The Office of Consumer Affairs provides a number of resources to deal with consumer complaints and the legal issues that can surround them.

www.ic.gc.ca/epic/site/oca-bc.nsf/en/h_ca02213e.html

Electronic Commerce

"The Canadian Code of Practice for Consumer Protection in Electronic Commerce" explains the code and its implementation principles for merchants doing business online.

"Your Internet Business—Earning Consumer Trust" provides online merchants with ways to protect consumers and earn their trust.

www.ic.gc.ca/epic/site/oca-bc.nsf/en/h_ca02214e.html

Identity Theft

"Business Identity Theft Kit" provides information on how to reduce the risk of identity theft for your business and customers, as well as what to do if a thief strikes.

"Identity Theft—Protect Your Business—Protect Your Customers" presents some information and useful tips on how to protect your business and clients from identity theft.

www.ic.gc.ca/epic/site/oca-bc.nsf/en/h_ca02306e.html

RCMP PHONEBUSTERS

Phonebusters is a partnership between the RCMP, the Competition Bureau of Canada, the Ontario Provincial Police, and the Government of Canada. The most up-to-date information on new scams (and older ones that keep finding unsuspecting targets) can be found here. Their motto is:

FRAUD. RECONGNIZE IT. REPORT IT. STOP IT.

Their site offers assistance with each of the above topics including statistics and resource materials. Most of the information relates to personal scams including the new emergency cash phone scam, warranty sales call scams, Bell Canada scams, etc.

www.phonebusters.com/english/index.html

Additional information can be obtained directly from the RCMP website:

www.rcmp-grc.gc.ca/scams/index_e.htm

FRAUD INFORMATION CENTRE AND SCAMS AGAINST BUSINESSES

This is the home of the National Consumers League Fraud Centre. They answer frequently asked questions and cover telemarketing fraud, Internet fraud, counterfeit drugs, and scams against the elderly. For small business, they provide information on the following fraud issues, detailed and explained below:

- Advertising materials—buying advertising in print material with very limited distribution
- Bogus invoices—invoices billed for things you did not order or receive
- Calling card charges—fraudulent long distance calls

made on your calling card
- Charitable solicitations—donations to charities where the majority of funds collected are for administration rather than charity
- Cramming—phone charges that are added unbeknownst to the client
- Fax fraud—fax requests for business information that requires you to incur a *substantial* long distance charge
- Internet services—solicitations to assist you with your website where funds are collected, but services are never obtained
- Loan scams—advance fees are collected for business loans that you will never obtain
- Nigerian money offers—claims reported to be from the Nigerian government where they require your bank account number to move funds out of the country
- Pager scams—messages left purporting to be urgent encouraging you to call back an international phone number and later are charged exorbitant long distance fees.
- Paper pirates and toner phoner—calls or emails supposedly from your usual supplier (not so) selling paper, printer or other products (you pay high costs and/or never get what you ordered)
- Pay-per-call scams—phone bills for 1-800, 1-900 or other international calls that you never agreed to
- PBX phone scams—a scam for integrated telephone systems, where you are asked by a caller to press #90 for a variety of reasons and find out you have opened up your phone system to unauthorized long distance calling by third parties
- Prize promotions—your business has qualified to receive a prize, you just need to buy hundreds of cheap key chains (or whatever) with your business logo. The "prize"

is cheap and basically worthless.
- Slamming—when your telephone service is switched to another carrier (with significantly higher charges) without your authorization
- The site also include tips for online auctions. *www.fraud.org/scamsagainstbusinesses/bizscams.htm*

GOVERNMENT OF CANADA
Canada Business Services for Entrepreneurs

The Canada Business Network is a government service for all types of businesses, including start-ups. They offer a one-stop access point for the many government organizations that administer small business services, programs, and regulations.

Information they provide covers:

- Starting a business
- Financing
- Taxes and GST
- Hiring and firing
- Exporting and importing
- Research and statistics
- Selling to government
- E-business and innovation
- Regulations, licences, and permits

In addition to covering these important topics the organization offers Fraud Awareness Info-Guides on identity theft, bad cheque control, and preventing theft.

Canada Business Services for Entrepreneurs can be found at: *www.canadabusiness.ca/gol/cbec/site.nsf/en/index.html*

OFFICE OF THE SUPERINTENDENT OF FINANCIAL INSTITUTIONS

The Office of the Superintendent of Financial Institution's mandate is to supervise all financial institutions, pension plans, and life insurance companies doing business in Canada. They maintain a "beware of scams" section and a "warning notice" section. The warning notices lists the names of entities purporting to be financial or insurance companies that they believe could be a concern to the business community and the public. Specific business names are listed that have been linked to complaints of fraudulent or illegal activities.

They also provide information on various types of scams or frauds attempted through emails published on the Internet, or in other media. Read about a current "locked in" RRSP scam and Ontario Securities Commission investor alerts. *www.osfi-bsif.gc.ca/osfi/*

ONGUARD ONLINE/YOUR SAFETY NET

The OnGuardOnline.gov website advises that they "provide practical tips from the U.S. Federal Government and the technology industry to help you be on guard against Internet fraud, secure your computer, and protect your personal information." They provide some additional computer fraud information from a U.S. focus, including cross-border scams, P2P, VoIP, and wireless security. *www.onguardonline.gov*

CANADA POST

Canada Post's corporate security division works with the RCMP and Canada Customs to seize and destroy Nigerian advance fee fraud letters. Not only are the letters part of an ongoing worldwide scam—even the stamps are counterfeit!

Their fraud protection advice can be found at:
www.canadapost.ca/help/fraud-e.asp

RETAIL COUNCIL OF CANADA

The Retail Council of Canada is a not-for-profit organization representing storefront sales businesses across Canada. They provide members with education, training, and best practices information.
www.retailcouncil.org/advocacy/lp/

TRANSUNION CANADA

TransUnion is a credit and information management organization. Their website states that they maintain more than 20 million consumer credit bureau files in their database (in 25 countries). If you become a member of the organization they offer small business solutions for:

- Risk management
- Collections management
- Data compromise assistance
- Credit reporting

Plus they offer further businesses specific assistance with fraud and identity detection tools, fraud analytics, high risk fraud alerts, and dynamic monitoring.
www.transunion.ca/ca/business/business_en.page

EQUIFAX

Equifax is another credit reporting agency. It is headquartered in Atlanta, Georgia.
www.equifax.com/home/en_ca

KPMG CANADA

KPMG is the Canadian arm of a worldwide audit, tax, forensic accounting, and business advisory company. They also have a "risk and resilience" practice to assist in protecting businesses against critical risks. They offer services both for large public and small private companies.

www.kpmg.ca/en/services/advisory/forensic/fraudRisk.ht ml

CANADIAN BANKERS ASSOCIATION

The Canadian Bankers Association is an organization that advocates on behalf of the banking industry with respect to public policies. They provide information on both fraud and security, as well as small business services.

www.cba.ca

BETTER BUSINESS BUREAU IN CANADA

The BBB is a not-for-profit agency financed by businesses. The goal of the organization is to solidify the relationship between business and the consumer by promoting ethical business practices. The main website provides links to all BBB information centres across Canada. You can search for information on businesses (whether BBB members or not) including:

* How long the company has been established
* The owner's name
* Business location
* History of complaints and resolutions

The BBB also offers your business dispute resolution for client complaints and fraud alerts.

www.ccbbb.ca

CBC NEWS *MARKETPLACE*

Marketplace is CBC's award winning consumer affairs television program.

www.cbc.ca/consumers/market/files/scams/

CANADIAN MARKETING ASSOCIATION

The Canadian Marketing Association is a non-profit members' organization that supports a business code of ethics and marketing education. They work with issues facing business marketing policies and practices in Canada such as consumer privacy, spam email, behavioural and mobile marketing, and fraud prevention. The organization also offers marketing resources and professional marketing certificates in:

• Customer insight through research and analytics
• Advertising and media
• Direct marketing
• E-Marketing
• Integrated branding
www.the-cma.org

INTERNET CRIME COMPLAINT CENTER (U.S.)

The Internet Crime Complaint Center (IC3) is a partnership between the Federal Bureau of Investigation (FBI), the National White Collar Crime Center (NW3C), and the Bureau of Justice Assistance (BJA).

While Canadians cannot use this service to lodge complaints (unless it is against a U.S. organization), the site offers a "Press Room" section that details current scam information i.e., the newest "hit man" emails, warnings on worms that are circulating, and updates for vishing and phishing schemes.

www.ic3.gov/media/default.aspx

SECURITIES COMMISSIONS ACROSS CANADA

Each province has a regulatory body whose mandate is to protect investors from unscrupulous sales agents using improper or fraudulent practices. If you or your business are investing funds, you should be aware of the various types of investment scams.

THE CANADIAN SECURITIES COMMISSION

Links to all provincial offices:

www.sedi.ca/sedi/help/english/public/external_links/cana dian_commision_contact_info.htm

A FEW SPECIFIC FRAUD INFORMATION LINKS

Ontario

The Ontario Securities Commission's website has information on recognizing investment scams and provides alerts.

www.osc.gov.on.ca/Investor/ScamsFraud/sf_index.jsp

Alberta

Investor tools: check first, scam stoppers, investors watch, courses, and resources.

www.albertasecurities.com/Pages/Default.aspx

New Brunswick

The New Brunswick Securities Commission has information on avoiding and reporting scams:

www.nbsc-cvmnb.ca/nbsc/

Nova Scotia

The Nova Scotia Securities Commission provides information on investment frauds and scams as well as Internet fraud.

www.gov.ns.ca/nssc/

GOVERNMENT OF CANADA PUBLIC SAFETY PORTAL

A link to public safety information and services in Canada. The website provides small business owners with information on:

- Bullying
- Criminal Activity/Policing
- Emergencies and Disasters
- Environmental Protection
- Family Home and Safety
- Financial Safety
- Health Protection
- Internet Safety
- National Safety and Security
- Product and Consumer Protection
- Recreational Safety
- School Safety
- Transportation and Travel Safety
- Workplace Safety

Public Safety Canada mandates

Emergency management—working to reduce the impact of natural disasters, industrial accidents, terrorism and computer viruses.

National security—responsible for policy development and advice to the Minister on matters of national security

Crime prevention—providing national leadership on effective and cost-effective ways to prevent and reduce crime

Law enforcement policy—develop appropriate national policies for new and evolving crime and border issues

Corrections policy—develop legislation and policies governing corrections, implementing innovative approaches to community justice, and providing research expertise and re-

sources to the corrections community
www.publicsafety.gc.ca/index-eng.aspx

GOVERNMENT OF CANADA

Twenty-five federal government departments working together to provide Canadians with a peaceful and safe society.
www.safecanada.ca/menu_e.asp
Alerts, advisories, and warnings are also available on the safety portal website.
www.safecanada.ca

ABC'S OF FRAUD

This site is a collaboration by the Office of Consumer Affairs (Industry Canada), Manitoba Consumers' Bureau, The Royal Canadian Mounted Police, the Mounted Police First Nations, Volunteer Toronto, Financial Services OmbudsNetwork, and HeadsUp.

On the site you can test how much you know about fraud with quizzes, learn about online scams, credit and debit card frauds, investment scams, and identity theft.
www.abcfraud.ca

10.
What's New: Up and Coming Protection

There are numerous financial and government organizations, along with other innovative businesses, working to combat fraud and theft from several different perspectives. From sophisticated computer security programs to new and improved high tech tracking systems, there are many new risk and fraud control products available for small business.

CREDIT AND BANK CHIP CARDS

You may have already started seeing some of these new security devices. The chip card, or smart card, was invented in the 1960s but gained popularity in several European countries during the 1990s. The chip is a small memory circuit that is embedded into the front of a plastic card. This is where your credit card or bank information will be held instead of the black magnetic strip on the reverse. The chip has superior fraud and security protection for your card's data—it is very difficult to copy. With the chip card, a signature will no longer be required for any credit card purchases. Validation of a charge is completed using a personal identification number (PIN).Visa, MasterCard, and American Express, along with several other credit providers, have embraced this technology and chip cards are now being issued across Canada. They began their extensive roll out in 2008. Due to the number of credit cards in existence, the transfer to the new chip cards will take a few years to complete. This also means that businesses need to update their Point-of-Sale (POS) terminals to be able to read the microchips. It will undoubtedly take several years as well for every business to have the correct equipment installed—think of how many businesses accept credit cards for payments! The cards will initially be manufactured with both the chip feature and the magnetic strip in order for transactions to be possible in either type of POS terminal. Once all businesses have been changed over the magnetic strip will no longer be built into the cards. All of the major banks will also be converting their particular in branch and telephone banking client cards to this new technology.

The hand-held chip card readers are available in many restaurants. You should know that when you are provided with your new chip enabled Visa or MasterCard you will also be receiving a new PIN. For chip cards, the PIN will be required right away for any of the merchants whose POS equipment has been converted. These cards will be a great benefit to small businesses for face-to-face client transactions. Any transaction where a PIN is used will have a decreased possibility of being fraudulent. While chip cards will be more secure than the current cards, as long as the magnetic strip remains and a signature continues to be obtained for a sale, the possibility of fraud will remain as it is today. Chip cards will not protect against fraudulent Internet transactions.

See Visa, MasterCard, or American Express' websites for information on chip cards.

RADIO FREQUENCY IDENTIFICATION TAGS (RFID)

The above chip card transformation is one of several other tracking and security measures now available via Radio Frequency Identification Tags.

RFID has three components:

- Firstly, there is the RFID "tag." This is a small computer chip that stores various amounts of information. The information the tag holds can be whatever you want it to be. It could be that the tag identifies a teapot and that it's specifically number 20 of 30 identical teapots that you have in stock. These tags can be fastened directly to the inventory item, the item's packaging, or to plastic cards that are attached in the same way UPC codes now are. The tags can also be inserted inside an item such as for animal identification purposes. For instance, you can maintain and manage information related to a cat, dog, or horse such as gender, birth date, parentage, and health vaccinations received. The tag also has the ability to transmit whatever information it holds to a receiver.

- The second component is an RFID "reader" or data receiver. The receiver asks the tag for the information it is holding and the data is sent to the receiver via a transponder chip in the tag. The receiver could be a hand-held wand or box that is waved over the tag by an employee. In stores we now see UPC code readers being waved over items we are purchasing. This may seem the same, but it isn't exactly. In the case of the UPC code, the scanner reads only a limited amount of information. It determines that the unit is a particular brand of teapot that costs $9.99 and that's all. All of the teapots have the same UPC code. The RFID chip tag contains much more detailed information. Not only does the tag tell you that it is a particular teapot that costs $9.99, it will also tell you that it's teapot number nine of the 20 that were put on the shelf for sale. Further, it also could let you know that the teapot was purchased from the Teapot Company in Moncton, New Brunswick, at a wholesale cost of $6.59 and that it arrived in your warehouse only two days ago. A UPC code will not tell you any of that. RFID readers can also be stationary units where the item itself must pass nearby, such as on a conveyor belt, in order for the information to be transmitted. Your manufacturing business will not only be able to count exactly how many bread boxes were made on a particular day but perhaps, also, which employee assembled or packaged it and the exact date and time of day bread box number 4,025 was made. The tag chip usually needs to be within a fairly close range (one to three metres) for the reader to receive the data. There are other readers that are capable of picking up RFID chip transmissions for further distances. These readers store the accumulated data from all of the tags read.

•   Thirdly, there is a computer/computer software program that accesses the RFID reader data and analyses the information gathered. How about those teapots? Eighteen of the 20 were sold within two days of arriving. They're a hot selling item—time to order more right away. You may also be able to see that this is the first time you have ordered from the Teapot Company. If their teapots are a hot item, maybe you should investigate other related products that they manufacture. What about the bread boxes? Lately, you have been receiving a lot of returned products from several different retailers due to workmanship defects. The RFID tags tell you that they were all assembled within the last month by one specific employee.

RFID is actually an older technology that was used back in WWII to track airplanes. Aircraft still use the same technology today; however, many new and creative uses have been developed from the existing knowledge. Here are some of the current applications:

- animal identification ("chipping" you cat or dog)
- inventory shipment tracking
- retail sales tracking
- pass cards used to take public transportation (prepaid fares)
- prepaid business loyalty cards (like in coffee shops)
- pass card entry for offices or buildings
- automated car lock and car ignition keys
- toll highway car identification and billing
- gas stations fast pay cards (that just have to be swiped for billing purposes)
- retaining passport data

In 2001, the Canadian Food Inspection Agency mandated RFID tags to track cattle, bison, and sheep movement for food safety purposes. The tags allow the tracking of animals for health related issues such as determining the origin of an identified case of mad cow disease—whether discovered in one individual or for a larger outbreak.

As well, some large retailers have started to request that their suppliers provide RFID tracking for any inventory or supplies that they purchase. The Electronic Product Code (EPC) may be on its way to eventually replacing the Universal Product Code (UPC). Today UPC bar codes must be read individually—each item must be scanned separately. RFID systems have been tested where entire grocery carts of items have been scanned in one sweep of the RFID reader, which then records the sale as a single transaction.

Other expanding uses for RFID technology? Where I live, RFID has been installed in the public library for book check out. This method of tracking should also work for any business that rents DVDs, cars, or any other type of equipment. The tag could record when the item left the store, who has it (name, address, and credit card number), rental fee, and when it's due back and if it was returned on time.

RFID is not the same as some other types of radio frequency tags that are used in retail stores today. Often CDs, computer discs, or other small, high priced items are tagged with a device that will activate an alarm should the article be removed from the store prior to the tag being deactivated by the sales clerk. The tags are also occasionally found on clothing. These are actually radio or acoustic tags used to combat theft. They do not identify the particular item at all but only cause an alarm to sound when the activated tag crosses through a particular area. These tags do not contain any data.

There are two different types of RFID tags. One type will not transmit any of the data it holds until the RFID reader "asks" for the information. This is called a passive tag. It has the ability to store only a small amount of data. The other type of RFID tag has its own internal power to transmit without needing the reader to request the information first. This is called an active tag. An active RFID has the ability to store much more information than a passive one. It can also transmit its data over a longer distance. The cost of the passive tag system is much lower than the active one.

Benefits of using RFID

Obviously, one of the primary benefits of RFID for small business is the tracking of inventory holdings. Imagine a system that has the potential to remind you when your stock of a product is getting low and needs to be reordered before the shelves are bare. Or that the shelf stock of a particular product is low, however, there are still ten packages sitting in your warehouse available to be moved up for sale in the store. The reverse can also be true. How many of your products have been sitting on the shelf too long and are not selling? Perhaps it's time for a sale to get rid of them. RFID technology can be used to assist you in understanding your clients' buying choices and habits. With RFID sales tracking you would be able to fine-tune your business product offerings quickly in order to save the costs of having merchandise sitting in the warehouse or on store shelves unsold. One day, perhaps, we might have an RFID system for our own home refrigerators. Everything that goes into or out of the fridge is recorded and tracked without any extra work; just a quick scan in and out. On Saturday morning the system will tell you what you have and what you need to buy—a pre-determined personal shopping list without having to actually look inside.

If the products that you purchased are already RFID tagged, it would take only a few short minutes to scan entire shipments to confirm that you have received everything that you ordered—without even opening the boxes. The time cost savings for employees verifying that the correct numbers of products were delivered could be significant. (Of course, there could be RFID transponders in the boxes not attached to anything—that's a potential up and coming fraud issue.)

Recently other new and inventive ideas have come out of RFID technology. In Ontario, the system is currently in use at a family resort. Wristbands provided unlock room doors and allow food, beverages, and souvenirs to be "purchased" with the swipe of the wrist. The wristband has the option of being "loaded" with cash from a credit card advance or attached to the room invoice. At least one European family theme park has implemented RFID technology in wristbands that are rented to parents of young children. If the child should become lost, the band can be scanned for parental information (which includes the parent's cellphone number or other contact information).

You can see that while small businesses will benefit

greatly from RFID technology, its uses go beyond that to many other unique applications. In some atypical situations, RFID units have actually been used for human tracking purposes. There have been documented situations where the chips were implanted into an employee's hand or arm to control access to a secure room. Implantation of a chip into a human body has also occurred in a beach club for the purpose of access to an exclusive VIP area and to charge drinks and food. Some current applications are a little bizarre perhaps (these people did agree to having the chips implanted), but there are many great ideas in use today for RFID technology.

Some of the other recent uses identified for RFID technology:

- elder care facilities with RFID chipped clothing in order to identify the specific owners
- tracking dairy farm milk production
- RFID hardware used to monitor temperature and humidity at a winery
- a national fitness firm has introduced an automated personal training system using RFID

For more interesting information on uses for RFID technology, visit the RFID journal at *www.rfidjournal.com*

What's not to like about RFID?

Small business can benefit from RFID in various ways today with further uses currently in development and/or in testing phases. It should be noted, however, that the issue of consumer privacy has been raised on several occasions by various organizations.

So far, for retail sales, RFID has been used generally for tracking shipments per box or skid as opposed to being assigned to each single product. Large scale tagging of single objects remains costly. If we get to a time where individual items are being tagged, another potential problem is related to the type and amount of information that can be held on the tag. Today it is normally minimal product based identification details. RFID technology has the potential to link the specific sale of an item to an individual client—particularly if they use a credit card to purchase the item or present a loyalty card at the time of sale. In these cases there could be the ability for the RFID reader to record and match the tag information to a specific client transaction. Considering the current privacy laws in Canada, there is a concern that such collection of data could be concealed and/or misused.

As well, if individual items have RFID tags, will the tag continue to remain active (and readable) after the sale has been completed? Often this is the case. What might be the consequences for the buyer of a cell phone with an RFID tag that was not removed when entering or exiting the store days or weeks after the purchase?

What if you've just loaded your subway transit card with fares and are standing near an RFID reader? Maybe one that you can't see—one that thieves have made to steal whatever data your card may contain. Could your fares be stolen and transferred to another card? Yes, the potential is there.

There may also be recycling issues with the assortment of metal products that are used to manufacture RDIF tags, which would likely be disposed of in normal household garbage. If the tags become attached to all types of individual consumer products the amount of waste may become an issue.

Many people are not aware that RFID technology is already in wide use. As you can see, its current applications are numerous and growing. This technology could have a significant impact on all of our personal and business lives in the years ahead. As alternative applications are developed and implementation becomes more economical, small businesses will have brand new opportunities to better manage their inventory, sales, and profits. There are, as mentioned, some significant potential technological issues with respect to data security and also the environment that still need to be addressed and overcome. These concerns are currently being explored by federal and provincial government agencies, including many private enterprises.

BIOMETRICS

Over the past few years, there has been a surge in the use of various biometric identification systems: iris, retina, fingerprint and hand scanning for identification purposes, or facial and voice recognition programs. The systems can work one of two ways: By identifying an unknown person by matching data received to existing data held on file or verifying the identity of a known person.

Various countries including the U.S., the United Kingdom, and many in the European Union are now using biometric systems for passports and security clearance cards. Passport Canada is in the process of developing their own system.

The Canada Border Services Agency currently uses digital fingerprint equipment to scan and forward prints to the RCMP. The system allows them faster ID confirmation.

Canada also has iris scanners for the NEXUS and CANPASS air programs. NEXUS allows pre-screened frequent travellers faster crossing over the Canada and U.S. borders. CANPASS is the same pass used for air travel.

Pre-screened and approved travellers will receive a membership ID card and be allowed a fast track through security clearances via automated self-serve kiosks at airports and dedicated land border crossing lanes. The membership card can be used as an alternative to a passport for all Canada/U.S. travel. All applications require approval by both the Canadian and U.S. governments. There is a paper-based or online application plus a face-to-face interview. If approved, there will be a digital picture taken of your irises and your face for future identification purposes. Both application processing and membership fees apply for this service.

Citizenship and Immigration Canada conducted a field trial using fingerprint and facial biometrics. Out of 18,264 visa applications, 394 were found to be duplications. Their match rate was highly successful.

The purpose of the field trial was to determine what effect biometric requirements would have on the integrity of our citizenship and immigration programs, including the effect on customer service and procedures. The trial was run for six months at two immigration offices abroad and a Canadian refugee centre. During the trial, applicants at these locations were subject to biometric photos and fingerprinting. Their passports also contained a microchip to identify them as being a participant in the project. The results of the test of approximately 18,000 found that 2.1% of the applications were duplications. Some persons applied a second, third, or fourth time after being rejected repeatedly. The results included one person who committed identity fraud by applying under someone else's name and two that were refused visas and then travelled to Canada anyway with improper or fraudulent documents using their real names. In nine cases, the people were issued visas and later claimed refugee protection. In general, the results of the trial considered biometric identification to be a positive step towards effectively confirming a person's identity and detecting fraud.

See their trial results:

Biometrics Field Trial Evaluation Report

Program Integrity—Usefulness of Biometrics in Strengthening Identity Management and in Detecting Fraud
www.cic.gc.ca/english/resources/publications/biometrics-eval/index.asp

This type of protection is also now available to any business if you have reason for it and think the cost is warranted. Biometric security is definitely not just for science fiction movies any more!

Conclusion

No one expects that a small business will use all of the suggestions described here!

You should, nonetheless, be aware of what the various types of business operating risks can be and implement the protections you believe suit your circumstances best.

The costs of fraud, in fact, can be much higher than the actual loss itself when you consider:

- the cash value of the loss
- management costs (the time you take out of your main duties to deal with the issue—perhaps including notifying the police)
- extra accounting fees to verify what happened
- legal costs to attempt recovery
- potential for further loss of business when your other clients find out what happened and lose trust in your product, services, or business management
- hiring and re-training someone new if the problem involved employees

Starting up and running a business requires a person to have many diverse attributes and some specialized knowledge, for example, business development ability, sales and marketing know-how, finance and cost planning, not to mention that special talent or product you have to sell. It would be a good idea to make use of the many community colleges that offer small business training and guidance for areas in which you do not have a strong background. In addition, there is also a vast assortment of books and seminars available covering many types of business issues and concerns. Use the ones that you think will benefit you and your business the most.

I hope that you have not found the information outlined here to be overly pessimistic towards starting or running a small business. While owning your own business can occasionally be very stressful, there are usually many opportunities for you to have positive and enriching experiences—both financial and otherwise. Successful small business management is a juggling act that requires knowledge, determination, perseverance, and perhaps a tiny bit of luck. While I have described a variety of areas where a business can get into financial trouble and even fail, the purpose of outlining these issues is to highlight the preventative actions that can be taken, hopefully to preclude you from having the unfortunate experience of dealing with these issues. I have provided various action plans that will assist you in structuring your company and its practices in such a way as to enhance you business' long-term success. You must remember though, not only do you need to set up the checks and balances that your specific business should have, you also need to ensure that you are diligent in managing and following up on whichever protection policies you have established.

In August 2008, the United States Justice Department uncovered a global fraud coalition between persons in the U.S., Estonia, Ukraine, China, and Belarus. Using Wi-Fi, the thieves had hacked into nine major U.S. department store databases and stole forty million credit and debit card numbers.

www.usdoj.gov/opa/pr/2008/August/08-ag-689.html

We can certainly expect more of that. Fraud experts believe that the upcoming years will be especially challenging for fighting cybercrime and identity theft. New and better technology is spreading further and is available for lower costs than ever before. This has given many, who previously could not afford the equipment, the ability to compete with the fraud professionals to steal your money. With the current economic troubles around the world, the experts expect increasingly sophisticated international fraud schemes to emerge. Technology experts believe there will be ten times more malware deployed to steal personal information than is already in use. I expect also that many decent individuals, with new financial problems, will become pressured to defraud if given the opportunity. With respect to small business scams, the scammers are always changing and adapting to circumstances and therefore so should you. Please take some additional time to review the Reference section. I've included some links that will provide you names of organizations with information and ideas to combat financial fraud, plus a few others that will keep you up-to-date on new personal and small business scams. I have made every attempt to include accurate URLs.

For your best chance of long-term success, you should never stop learning about your business, your marketplace, and your clients (both good and bad aspects of them). Your ability to circumvent a major fraud depends on ensuring you have instituted the fraud prevention controls your company needs. It's equally essential that you and your organization maintain a strong preventative awareness and culture of fraud prevention.

A special thank you to Jeremy Carr, whose insight into computer operations and security was invaluable to this book.

References and Additional Information

A reasonable effort has gone into identifying reliable web addresses to provide further resources relative to small business fraud and risk. Nevertheless, as always, you must ensure that any information obtained through online sources is confirmed trustworthy before relying on it.

ACCOUNTANTS, BOOKKEEPERS, AND LAWYERS: FIND AN ACCOUNTANT (A FEW OF MANY CHOICES)

General
www.professionalreferrals.ca/

Alberta
www.icaa.ab.ca/databases/

British Columbia and Yukon
blog.gethelp.ca/2006/06/20/finding-an-accountant-in-bc/
or
www2.cga-bc.org/members/findacga/index.shtml

Manitoba
www.mycgawebservices.org/ebusiness/Directories/Find-AFirm/Browse.aspx

New Brunswick
www.cga-nb.org/cga/index.aspx?tid=1380&pid=1007

Newfoundland and Labrador
www.cganl.org/cga/index.aspx

Nova Scotia

www.cga-ns.org/content/Find_a_CGA_Firm

Ontario

*www.cga-ontario.org/applications/accountantreferral
/default.aspx* or *www.icao.on.ca/public/apps/cafirm/cafirm.
aspx*

Quebec

*www.cga-quebec.org/pls/htmldb/f?p=9105:23:
11496559102279695178*

CANADIAN ACCOUNTING AND/OR FINANCIAL ASSOCIATIONS

Canadian Institute of Chartered Accountants
www.cica.ca/index.cfm?ci_id=17150&la_id=1

Canadian Payroll Association
www.payroll.ca/

Canadian Property Tax Association
cpta.org/

Canadian Tax Foundation
www.ctf.ca/

Canadian Taxpayers Federation
www.taxpayer.com/taxpayer/home1

Certified General Accountants' Association of Canada
www.cga-canada.org/en-ca/Pages/default.aspx

Certified Management Accountants of Canada
www.cma-canada.org/

Comptables agréés du Québec
ocaq.qc.ca/

Guild of Industrial, Commercial and Institutional Accountants
www.guildoficia.ca/

Registered Public Accountants Association of Alberta
www.rpaa.org/

Society of Certified Management Accountants of Canada
www.cma-canada.org/index.cfm/ci_id/1633/la_id/1.htm

Society of Professional Accountants of Canada
www.professionalaccountant.org/SPAC/main/index.jsp

ASSOCIATION OF CERTIFIED FRAUD EXAMINERS
eweb.acfe.com

LOCATE A BOOKKEEPER
www.c-b-a.ca/members.htm

SEARCH FOR A LAWYER THROUGH PROVINCIAL LAW SOCIETIES
Alberta:
www.lawsocietyalberta.com/publicservices/lawyerReferralService.cfm

British Columbia
www.lawsociety.bc.ca/public/finding_lawyer.html

Manitoba
www.lawsociety.mb.ca/lookup/lawyer_look_up.asp

New Brunswick
www.lawsociety-barreau.nb.ca

Newfoundland and Labrador
www.lawsociety.nf.ca/

Northwest Territories
www.lawsociety.nt.ca

Nova Scotia
www.nsbs.ns.ca/legal_dir_home.htm

Nunavut
lawsociety.nu.ca/members.html

Ontario
www.lsuc.on.ca

Prince Edward Island
www.lspei.pe.ca/members.php

Quebec
www.barreau.qc.ca/repertoire/

Saskatchewan
www.lawsociety.sk.ca/members/memberquery.htm

Yukon
www.lawsocietyyukon.com/referral.php

BANK OF CANADA

"Fight Fraud on the Front Lines: A Retailers Guide"
www.bankofcanada.ca/en/banknotes/retail.html

CANADA'S ANTI-MONEY LAUNDERING AND ANTI-TERRORIST FINANCING INITIATIVE

www.fintrac.gc.ca/fintrac-canafe/antimltf-eng.asp

CANADIAN PAYMENTS ASSOCIATION

The Canadian Payments Association was established in 1980 by Parliament. The non-profit organization manages the clearing and settlement system between financial institutions in Canada. They process all cheques, transfers, deposits, debits, and other payments moving between the banks. Their website claims that "on average, some 22 million payment items, representing $203 billion in transactions, were cleared and settled through the CPA's systems each business day during 2007." On the website are details on how a cheque clears your account and includes additional information on when a cheque can be returned and debited back to your account. The site also includes information on your rights with respect to PADs (pre-authorized debits) and holds on cheques being deposited.

www.cdnpay.ca

CANADA REVENUE AGENCY

The Canada Revenue Agency offers tips on tax preparer fraud. Their criminal investigation program handles cases of tax evasion and tax fraud against individuals, companies, and tax preparers. You should be aware that you are ultimately responsible for all tax returns filed in your name. Fudging your income or expenses is considered tax fraud. Failure to file a tax return for yourself or your business is considered tax evasion. If you are caught and convicted of tax fraud or tax evasion you can be levied a hefty fine and in some cases receive a jail term. Your name and case information will also be added to the Revenue Canada website for others to see.

www.cra-arc.gc.ca/nwsrm/

DEPARTMENT OF JUSTICE CANADA: *CANADA LABOUR CODE*

laws.justice.gc.ca/en/L-2

FRAUD PUBLICATIONS

Fraud Magazine: *www.fraud-magazine.com/default.aspx*

The Association of Certified Fraud Examiners. *The Small Business Fraud Prevention Manual.* Austin: ACFE, 2004.

LIST OF INSURANCE COMPANIES AUTHORIZED TO CARRY ON BUSINESS IN CANADA UNDER THE *INSURANCE COMPANIES ACT*

Office of the Superintendent of Financial Institutions of Canada (OSFI)

www.osfi-bsif.gc.ca/osfi/index_e.aspx?ArticleID=552

PERSONAL INFORMATION PROTECTION AND ELECTRONIC DOCUMENTS ACT (PIPEDA):

Information for Businesses:

www.privcom.gc.ca/bus/index_e.asp

TELEPHONE FRAUD

Bell.ca advises that international telecommunications fraud costs $12 billion per year, with Canada accounting for $30 million of that total. Read their warnings about Internet auto-diallers and toll/long distance frauds.

www.bell.ca/shopping/PrsShpPns_Lng_Fraud.page

Telus.com notes that telephone scams and long distance

abuse are big business in North America. Read about slamming and switching, scams, and toll frauds along with modem hijacking.

about.telus.com/publicpolicy/scamsandfraud.html

Your particular provider may also offer additional security warnings and protection advice.

Business Fraud and Loss Avoidance Checklist

Setting Up a Business

- Have you discussed your new business proposal with a lawyer and an accountant?
- Will the business be a sole ownership, partnership, or corporation?
- If there are partners, how many will there be? Will there be a legal partnership agreement in place?
- Will there be a "chart" of responsibility and authority for each partner? Who will have the ability to override rules that have been set up and under what circumstances? If there is no chart, how will needed changes to the business operations be dealt with?
- Do you have a complete business plan including initial funding requirements, initial sales and income estimates, and projected future growth financial needs?
- How often will you review your business performance against your original plans? How often will business goals be reviewed?
- Is there sufficient life and business insurance in place to cover unexpected situations?
- Will you have an anti-fraud business plan? How will you manage and support it? How will you determine if it is working or not?

Setting Up a Business Bank Account

- Who will have authority to sign on the account? Who will control the bank cheques? Who will have responsibility for securing the daily client payments (cheques/cash/credit)? Who will make the bank deposits?
- Do you fully understand what banking services you have and the account agreement that you signed?
- Who will have control of balancing or validating the bank account statement monthly?
- Are you aware of any personal liability associated with the business account or business loans that you have?

Setting Up an Office or Warehouse

- How critical are the office equipment, the computer system, or the warehouse inventory? Is your security adequate to cover the assets' true value?
- Who will have access to the office or warehouse? Who will have their own key or pass?
- Do you have a plan for how you will keep business and client information secured?
- How will you manage and secure computer access and usage?
- Who will manage the list of vendors that the business will be using? What criteria will you use to choose which ones you will use? How often will you review the list?
- Can you ensure separation of duties (i.e., accounts payable, accounts receivable, making bank deposits)? How often and by whom will these staff duties be checked?
- Will there be internal audit checks in accounting and warehousing? What type of checks will there be and when will they be performed? Will there be a review of sales information, accounts receivable, and accounts

payables for data manipulation?

- Will you have a customer complaint process?
- Do you have an actual plan for emergencies like fire; verbal or physical threats from employees, employees' families, clients, vendors; power failures; and armed robberies?
- What personal safety features will you ensure the business location has? (Fire extinguishers, mapped building emergency exit routes, emergency medical supplies.)

Selecting a Bookkeeper, Accountant, or Lawyer

- How many references do you have?
- Have you checked with their professional societies to see if they are members in good standing?
- Have you checked the Better Business Bureau to see if any complaints have been registered against their business or firm?
- Have you met with each of them to discuss you business requirements prior to choosing one?

Dealing with Employees

- Who will be responsible for hiring? Will background checks be completed for all staff?
- Will each position have a job description? Who will train staff with respect to their duties and responsibilities?
- Will you support an ethical office environment? Will you have written policies in place re: behaviours towards coworkers and clients, fairness, fraud, theft, accepting gifts from suppliers, etc.? Will you have employees read and sign as acknowledgement of their understanding of the policies? How will the policies be enforced and by whom?
- Will you support staff in reporting fraud directly to you

or through an outside organization hired by the company? What will the process be?

- What training will you have available to ensure all staff are aware of your employment guidelines? Will they be required to re-train on a regular basis as a reminder? How often might that be?

- Do you know what the warning signs or indications are that an employee may be committing fraud? How will you be alerted to any unusual activities or behaviours of staff?

- If an employee leaves the company, will you have a procedure in place to immediately remove their access to all systems, buildings, files, equipment or vehicles?

- Will you enforce mandatory vacations and cross training?

- How will you ensure employees' activities are not in conflict of interest with your business? (For example, if a relationship develops between a customer or vendor and an employee which might influence the employee's actions.)

- Who will have expense accounts? For what purpose? With what limit? How will the charges be validated?

- If you pay employees by commission, how will you ensuring that all sales generated are legitimate?

- What will your employee discipline policies be? Firing policies?

- How will you evaluate your employees' work?

Dealing with Clients
- Will checks be done before granting credit to a client (including cashing personal cheques)? What will the checks be? Who will be responsible for completing the checks? Who will be responsible for collecting any bad debts?

- What about your top clients—what plan do you have to keep them? Will you have a sufficient client base so that

losing a few customers will not devastate the business?
- Will staff be trained in fraud detection for client credit card and cash transactions?
- How will your employees know what the latest small business scams are and how to avoid getting caught up in one?

How will you ensure that all of the fraud, loss avoidance, and security practices that you put into place are kept up-to-date?

Index

cramming, 177
Credit Bureau, 60, 83, 112, 115, 180

denial of service (DoS) attacks, 164
Department of Justice Canada, 81, 207
deposit acceleration, 31
direct deposit, 31
Dr. Phil, 138-140

electronic product code (EPC), 190
Equifax, 112, 132, 180
equipment
    leasing, 114-116
    See also *security*

Financial Services OmbudsNetwork, 185
FINTRAC, 34-36, 206
Fraud Magazine, 207
Fraud Prevention Forum (FPF), 172, 174

general partnership, 19-20
global positioning system (GPS), 48
gross earnings insurance, 16
gross profits insurance, 16
GST, 18, 178

incorporation, 14, 21
Industry Canada, 174
insurance
    business interruption , 16, 17, 53
    gross earnings, 16
    gross profit, 16
    key persons, 20

office, 53-54
Internet Crime Complaint Center, 182
inventory, 54-56

key persons insurance, 20
KPMG Canada, 182

letters of credit, 32
limited partnership, 19-20

malware, 59, 162-164, 200
    adware, 163-165
    spyware, 163, 164
Manitoba Consumers' Bureau, 186
MasterCard, 186, 187
merchant services, 33, 104, 105, 114
money laundering, 8, 34-36, 206

NEXUS, 195
non-sufficient funds (NSF), 37-39, 107, 113, 149, 160, 174-176, 179

Office of Consumer Affairs (OCA), 175
Office of the Privacy Commissioner of Canada, 60, 63
Office of the Superintendent of Financial Institutions (OSFI), 179
OnGuardOnline, 179
Ontario Provincial Police (OPP), 125, 177
Ontario Securities Commission (OSC), 179, 183

partnerships, 14, 19-20
Passport Canada, 195